# Practical Convolutional Networks

Implement advanced deep learning models using Python

**Mohit Sewak**
**Md. Rezaul Karim**
**Pradeep Pujari**

BIRMINGHAM - MUMBAI

# Practical Convolutional Neural Networks

**Commissioning Editor:** Sunith Shetty
**Acquisition Editor:** Vinay Argekar
**Content Development Editor:** Cheryl Dsa
**Technical Editor:** Sagar Sawant
**Copy Editor:** Vikrant Phadke, Safis Editing
**Project Coordinator:** Nidhi Joshi
**Proofreader:** Safis Editing
**Indexer:** Tejal Daruwale Soni
**Graphics:** Tania Dutta
**Production Coordinator:** Arvindkumar Gupta

First published: February 2018

Production reference: 1230218

Published by Packt Publishing Ltd.
Livery Place
35 Livery Street
Birmingham
B3 2PB, UK.

ISBN 978-1-78839-230-3

www.packtpub.com

`mapt.io`

Mapt is an online digital library that gives you full access to over 5,000 books and videos, as well as industry leading tools to help you plan your personal development and advance your career. For more information, please visit our website.

# Why subscribe?

- Spend less time learning and more time coding with practical eBooks and Videos from over 4,000 industry professionals

- Improve your learning with Skill Plans built especially for you

- Get a free eBook or video every month

- Mapt is fully searchable

- Copy and paste, print, and bookmark content

# PacktPub.com

Did you know that Packt offers eBook versions of every book published, with PDF and ePub files available? You can upgrade to the eBook version at `www.PacktPub.com` and as a print book customer, you are entitled to a discount on the eBook copy. Get in touch with us at `service@packtpub.com` for more details.

At `www.PacktPub.com`, you can also read a collection of free technical articles, sign up for a range of free newsletters, and receive exclusive discounts and offers on Packt books and eBooks.

# Contributors

## About the authors

**Mohit Sewak** is a senior cognitive data scientist with IBM, and a PhD scholar in AI and CS at BITS Pilani. He holds several patents and publications in AI, deep learning, and machine learning. He has been the lead data scientist for some very successful global AI/ ML software and industry solutions and was earlier engaged in solutioning and research for the Watson Cognitive Commerce product line. He has 14 years of rich experience in architecting and solutioning with TensorFlow, Torch, Caffe, Theano, Keras, Watson, and more.

**Md. Rezaul Karim** is a research scientist at Fraunhofer FIT, Germany. He is also a PhD candidate at RWTH Aachen University, Germany. Before joining FIT, he worked as a researcher at the Insight Center for Data Analytics, Ireland. He was a lead engineer at Samsung Electronics, Korea.

He has 9 years of R&D experience with C++, Java, R, Scala, and Python. He has published research papers on bioinformatics, big data, and deep learning. He has practical working experience with Spark, Zeppelin, Hadoop, Keras, Scikit-Learn, TensorFlow, Deeplearning4j, MXNet, and H2O.

**Pradeep Pujari** is machine learning engineer at Walmart Labs and a distinguished member of ACM. His core domain expertise is in information retrieval, machine learning, and natural language processing. In his free time, he loves exploring AI technologies, reading, and mentoring.

# About the reviewer

**Sumit Pal** is a published author with Apress. He has more than 22 years of experience in software, from start-ups to enterprises, and is an independent consultant working with big data, data visualization, and data science. He builds end-to-end data-driven analytic systems.

He has worked for Microsoft (SQLServer), Oracle (OLAP Kernel), and Verizon. He advises clients on their data architectures and build solutions in Spark and Scala. He has spoken at many conferences in North America and Europe and has developed a big data analyst training for Experfy. He has an MS and BS in computer science.

# Packt is searching for authors like you

If you're interested in becoming an author for Packt, please visit authors.packtpub.com and apply today. We have worked with thousands of developers and tech professionals, just like you, to help them share their insight with the global tech community. You can make a general application, apply for a specific hot topic that we are recruiting an author for, or submit your own idea.

# Table of Contents

# Preface

CNNs are revolutionizing several application domains, such as visual recognition systems, self-driving cars, medical discoveries, innovative e-commerce, and many more. This book gets you started with the building blocks of CNNs, while also guiding you through the best practices for implementing real-life CNN models and solutions. You will learn to create innovative solutions for image and video analytics to solve complex machine learning and computer vision problems.

This book starts with an overview of deep neural networks, with an example of image classification, and walks you through building your first CNN model. You will learn concepts such as transfer learning and autoencoders with CNN that will enable you to build very powerful models, even with limited supervised (labeled image) training data.

Later we build upon these learnings to achieve advanced vision-related algorithms and solutions for object detection, instance segmentation, generative (adversarial) networks, image captioning, attention mechanisms, and recurrent attention models for vision. Besides giving you hands-on experience with the most intriguing vision models and architectures, this book explores cutting-edge and very recent researches in the areas of CNN and computer vision. This enable the user to foresee the future in this field and quick-start their innovation journey using advanced CNN solutions.
By the end of this book, you should be ready to implement advanced, effective, and efficient CNN models in your professional projects or personal initiatives while working on complex images and video datasets.

# Who this book is for

This book is for data scientists, machine learning, and deep learning practitioners, and cognitive and artificial intelligence enthusiasts who want to move one step further in building CNNs. Get hands-on experience with extreme datasets and different CNN architectures to build efficient and smart ConvNet models. Basic knowledge of deep learning concepts and Python programming language is expected.

# What this book covers

Chapter 1, *Deep Neural Networks - Overview*, it gives a quick refresher of the science of deep neural networks and different frameworks that can be used to implement such networks, with the mathematics behind them.

Chapter 2, *Introduction to Convolutional Neural Networks*, it introduces the readers to convolutional neural networks and shows how deep learning can be used to extract insights from images.

Chapter 3, *Build Your First CNN and Performance Optimization*, constructs a simple CNN model for image classification from scratch, and explains how to tune hyperparameters and optimize training time and performance of CNNs for improved efficiency and accuracy respectively.

Chapter 4, *Popular CNN Model Architectures*, shows the advantages and working of different popular (and award winning) CNN architectures, how they differ from each other, and how to use them.

Chapter 5, *Transfer Learning*, teaches you to take an existing pretrained network and adapt it to a new and different dataset. There is also a custom classification problem for a real-life application using a technique called **transfer learning**.

Chapter 6, *Autoencoders for CNN*, introduces an unsupervised learning technique called **autoencoders**. We walk through different applications of autoencoders for CNN, such as image compression.

Chapter 7, *Object Detection and Instance Segmentation with CNN*, teaches the difference between object detection, instance segmentation, and image classification. We then learn multiple techniques for object detection and instance segmentation with CNNs.

Chapter 8, *GAN—Generating New Images with CNN*, explores generative CNN Networks, and then we combine them with our learned discriminative CNN networks to create new images with CNN/GAN.

Chapter 9, *Attention Mechanism for CNN and Visual Models*, teaches the intuition behind attention in deep learning and learn how attention-based models are used to implement some advanced solutions (image captioning and RAM). We also understand the different types of attention and the role of reinforcement learning with respect to the hard attention mechanism.

# To get the most out of this book

This book is focused on building CNNs with Python programming language. We have used Python version 2.7 (2x) to build various applications and the open source and enterprise-ready professional software using Python, Spyder, Anaconda, and PyCharm. Many of the examples are also compatible with Python 3x. As a good practice, we encourage users to use Python virtual environments for implementing these codes.

We focus on how to utilize various Python and deep learning libraries (Keras, TensorFlow, and Caffe) in the best possible way to build real-world applications. In that spirit, we have tried to keep all of the code as friendly and readable as possible. We feel that this will enable our readers to easily understand the code and readily use it in different scenarios.

# Download the example code files

You can download the example code files for this book from your account at `www.packtpub.com`. If you purchased this book elsewhere, you can visit `www.packtpub.com/support` and register to have the files emailed directly to you.

You can download the code files by following these steps:

1. Log in or register at `www.packtpub.com`.
2. Select the **SUPPORT** tab.
3. Click on **Code Downloads & Errata**.
4. Enter the name of the book in the **Search** box and follow the onscreen instructions.

Once the file is downloaded, please make sure that you unzip or extract the folder using the latest version of:

- WinRAR/7-Zip for Windows
- Zipeg/iZip/UnRarX for Mac
- 7-Zip/PeaZip for Linux

The code bundle for the book is also hosted on GitHub at `https://github.com/PacktPublishing/Practical-Convolutional-Neural-Networks`. In case there's an update to the code, it will be updated on the existing GitHub repository.

We also have other code bundles from our rich catalog of books and videos available at `https://github.com/PacktPublishing/`. Check them out!

# Download the color images

We also provide a PDF file that has color images of the screenshots/diagrams used in this book. You can download it here: http://www.packtpub.com/sites/default/files/downloads/PracticalConvolutionalNeuralNetworks_ColorImages.pdf.

# Conventions used

There are a number of text conventions used throughout this book.

CodeInText: Indicates code words in text, database table names, folder names, filenames, file extensions, pathnames, dummy URLs, user input, and Twitter handles. Here is an example: "Mount the downloaded WebStorm-10*.dmg disk image file as another disk in your system."

A block of code is set as follows:

```
import tensorflow as tf

#Creating TensorFlow object
hello_constant = tf.constant('Hello World!', name = 'hello_constant')
#Creating a session object for execution of the computational graph
with tf.Session() as sess:
```

When we wish to draw your attention to a particular part of a code block, the relevant lines or items are set in bold:

```
x = tf.subtract(1, 2,name=None) # -1
y = tf.multiply(2, 5,name=None) # 10
```

**Bold**: Indicates a new term, an important word, or words that you see onscreen. For example, words in menus or dialog boxes appear in the text like this. Here is an example: "Select **System info** from the **Administration** panel."

 Warnings or important notes appear like this.

 Tips and tricks appear like this.

# Get in touch

Feedback from our readers is always welcome.

**General feedback**: Email feedback@packtpub.com and mention the book title in the subject of your message. If you have questions about any aspect of this book, please email us at questions@packtpub.com.

**Errata**: Although we have taken every care to ensure the accuracy of our content, mistakes do happen. If you have found a mistake in this book, we would be grateful if you would report this to us. Please visit www.packtpub.com/submit-errata, selecting your book, clicking on the Errata Submission Form link, and entering the details.

**Piracy**: If you come across any illegal copies of our works in any form on the Internet, we would be grateful if you would provide us with the location address or website name. Please contact us at copyright@packtpub.com with a link to the material.

**If you are interested in becoming an author**: If there is a topic that you have expertise in and you are interested in either writing or contributing to a book, please visit authors.packtpub.com.

# Reviews

Please leave a review. Once you have read and used this book, why not leave a review on the site that you purchased it from? Potential readers can then see and use your unbiased opinion to make purchase decisions, we at Packt can understand what you think about our products, and our authors can see your feedback on their book. Thank you!

For more information about Packt, please visit packtpub.com.

# 1
# Deep Neural Networks – Overview

In the past few years, we have seen remarkable progress in the field of AI (deep learning). Today, deep learning is the cornerstone of many advanced technological applications, from self-driving cars to generating art and music. Scientists aim to help computers to not only understand speech but also speak in natural languages. Deep learning is a kind of machine learning method that is based on learning data representation as opposed to task-specific algorithms. Deep learning enables the computer to build complex concepts from simpler and smaller concepts. For example, a deep learning system recognizes the image of a person by combining lower label edges and corners and combines them into parts of the body in a hierarchical way. The day is not so far away when deep learning will be extended to applications that enable machines to think on their own.

In this chapter, we will cover the following topics:

- Building blocks of a neural network
- Introduction to TensorFlow
- Introduction to Keras
- Backpropagation

# Building blocks of a neural network

A neural network is made up of many artificial neurons. Is it a representation of the brain or is it a mathematical representation of some knowledge? Here, we will simply try to understand how a neural network is used in practice. A **convolutional neural network** (**CNN**) is a very special kind of multi-layer neural network. CNN is designed to recognize visual patterns directly from images with minimal processing. A graphical representation of this network is produced in the following image. The field of neural networks was originally inspired by the goal of modeling biological neural systems, but since then it has branched in different directions and has become a matter of engineering and attaining good results in machine learning tasks.

An artificial neuron is a function that takes an input and produces an output. The number of neurons that are used depends on the task at hand. It could be as low as two or as many as several thousands. There are numerous ways of connecting artificial neurons together to create a CNN. One such topology that is commonly used is known as a **feed-forward network**:

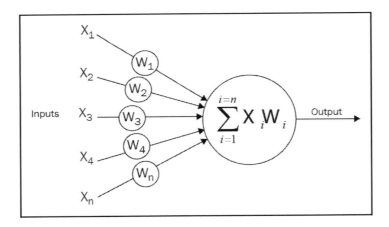

Each neuron receives inputs from other neurons. The effect of each input line on the neuron is controlled by the weight. The weight can be positive or negative. The entire neural network learns to perform useful computations for recognizing objects by understanding the language. Now, we can connect those neurons into a network known as a feed-forward network. This means that the neurons in each layer feed their output forward to the next layer until we get a final output. This can be written as follows:

$$w_1 x_1 + w_2 x_2 + \ldots + w_n x_n$$

$$\sum_{i=1}^{i=n} w_i x_i = w_1 x_1 + w_2 x_2 + \ldots + w_n x_n$$

The preceding forward-propagating neuron can be implemented as follows:

```python
import numpy as np
import math


class Neuron(object):
    def __init__(self):
        self.weights = np.array([1.0, 2.0])
        self.bias = 0.0
    def forward(self, inputs):
        """ Assuming that inputs and weights are 1-D numpy arrays and the
bias is a number """
        a_cell_sum = np.sum(inputs * self.weights) + self.bias
        result = 1.0 / (1.0 + math.exp(-a_cell_sum)) # This is the sigmoid
activation function
        return result
neuron = Neuron()
output = neuron.forward(np.array([1,1]))
print(output)
```

# Introduction to TensorFlow

TensorFlow is based on graph-based computation. Consider the following math expression, for example:

$$c=(a+b), d = b + 5,$$

$$e = c * d$$

In TensorFlow, this is represented as a computational graph, as shown here. This is powerful because computations are done in parallel:

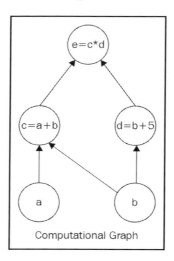

Computational Graph

# Installing TensorFlow

There are two easy ways to install TensorFlow:

- Using a virtual environment (recommended and described here)
- With a Docker image

# For macOS X/Linux variants

The following code snippet creates a Python virtual environment and installs TensorFlow in that environment. You should have Anaconda installed before you run this code:

```
#Creates a virtual environment named "tensorflow_env" assuming that python
3.7 version is already installed.
conda create -n tensorflow_env python=3.7
#Activate points to the environment named "tensorflow"
source activate tensorflow_env
conda install pandas matplotlib jupyter notebook scipy scikit-learn
#installs latest tensorflow version into environment tensorflow_env
pip3 install tensorflow
```

Please check out the latest updates on the official TensorFlow page, `https://www.tensorflow.org/install/`.

Try running the following code in your Python console to validate your installation. The console should print `Hello World!` if TensorFlow is installed and working:

```
import tensorflow as tf

#Creating TensorFlow object
hello_constant = tf.constant('Hello World!', name = 'hello_constant')
#Creating a session object for execution of the computational graph
with tf.Session() as sess:
    #Implementing the tf.constant operation in the session
    output = sess.run(hello_constant)
    print(output)
```

# TensorFlow basics

In TensorFlow, data isn't stored as integers, floats, strings, or other primitives. These values are encapsulated in an object called a **tensor**. It consists of a set of primitive values shaped into an array of any number of dimensions. The number of dimensions in a tensor is called its **rank**. In the preceding example, `hello_constant` is a constant string tensor with rank zero. A few more examples of constant tensors are as follows:

```
# A is an int32 tensor with rank = 0
A = tf.constant(123)
# B is an int32 tensor with dimension of 1 ( rank = 1 )
B = tf.constant([123,456,789])
# C is an int32 2- dimensional tensor
C = tf.constant([ [123,456,789], [222,333,444] ])
```

TensorFlow's core program is based on the idea of a computational graph. A computational graph is a directed graph consisting of the following two parts:

- Building a computational graph
- Running a computational graph

A computational graph executes within a **session**. A TensorFlow session is a runtime environment for the computational graph. It allocates the CPU or GPU and maintains the state of the TensorFlow runtime. The following code creates a session instance named `sess` using `tf.Session`. Then the `sess.run()` function evaluates the tensor and returns the results stored in the `output` variable. It finally prints as `Hello World!`:

```
with tf.Session() as sess:
    # Run the tf.constant operation in the session
    output = sess.run(hello_constant)
    print(output)
```

Using TensorBoard, we can visualize the graph. To run TensorBoard, use the following command:

```
tensorboard --logdir=path/to/log-directory
```

Let's create a piece of simple addition code as follows. Create a constant integer $x$ with value 5, set the value of a new variable $y$ after adding 5 to it, and print it:

```
constant_x = tf.constant(5, name='constant_x')
variable_y = tf.Variable(x + 5, name='variable_y')
print (variable_y)
```

The difference is that `variable_y` isn't given the current value of $x + 5$ as it should in Python code. Instead, it is an equation; that means, when `variable_y` is computed, take the value of $x$ at that point in time and add 5 to it. The computation of the value of `variable_y` is never actually performed in the preceding code. This piece of code actually belongs to the computational graph building section of a typical TensorFlow program. After running this, you'll get something like `<tensorflow.python.ops.variables.Variable object at 0x7f074bfd9ef0>` and not the actual value of `variable_y` as 10. To fix this, we have to execute the code section of the computational graph, which looks like this:

```
#initialize all variables
init = tf.global_variables_initializer()
# All variables are now initialized

with tf.Session() as sess:
    sess.run(init)
    print(sess.run(variable_y))
```

Here is the execution of some basic math functions, such as addition, subtraction, multiplication, and division with tensors. For more math functions, please refer to the documentation:

For TensorFlow math functions, go to `https://www.tensorflow.org/versions/r0.12/api_docs/python/math_ops/basic_math_functions`.

# Basic math with TensorFlow

The `tf.add()` function takes two numbers, two tensors, or one of each, and it returns their sum as a tensor:

```
Addition
x = tf.add(1, 2, name=None) # 3
```

Here's an example with subtraction and multiplication:

```
x = tf.subtract(1, 2,name=None) # -1
y = tf.multiply(2, 5,name=None) # 10
```

What if we want to use a non-constant? How to feed an input dataset to TensorFlow? For this, TensorFlow provides an API, `tf.placeholder()`, and uses `feed_dict`.

A `placeholder` is a variable that data is assigned to later in the `tf.session.run()` function. With the help of this, our operations can be created and we can build our computational graph without needing the data. Afterwards, this data is fed into the graph through these placeholders with the help of the `feed_dict` parameter in `tf.session.run()` to set the `placeholder` tensor. In the following example, the tensor `x` is set to the string `Hello World` before the session runs:

```
x = tf.placeholder(tf.string)

with tf.Session() as sess:
    output = sess.run(x, feed_dict={x: 'Hello World'})
```

It's also possible to set more than one tensor using `feed_dict`, as follows:

```
x = tf.placeholder(tf.string)
y = tf.placeholder(tf.int32, None)
z = tf.placeholder(tf.float32, None)

with tf.Session() as sess:
    output = sess.run(x, feed_dict={x: 'Welcome to CNN', y: 123, z:
123.45})
```

Placeholders can also allow storage of arrays with the help of multiple dimensions. Please see the following example:

```
import tensorflow as tf

x = tf.placeholder("float", [None, 3])
y = x * 2

with tf.Session() as session:
    input_data = [[1, 2, 3],
                  [4, 5, 6],]
    result = session.run(y, feed_dict={x: input_data})
    print(result)
```

This will throw an error as `ValueError: invalid literal for...` in cases where the data passed to the `feed_dict` parameter doesn't match the tensor type and can't be cast into the tensor type.

The `tf.truncated_normal()` function returns a tensor with random values from a normal distribution. This is mostly used for weight initialization in a network:

```
n_features = 5
n_labels = 2
weights = tf.truncated_normal((n_features, n_labels))
with tf.Session() as sess:
  print(sess.run(weights))
```

# Softmax in TensorFlow

The softmax function converts its inputs, known as **logit** or **logit scores**, to be between 0 and 1, and also normalizes the outputs so that they all sum up to 1. In other words, the softmax function turns your logits into probabilities. Mathematically, the softmax function is defined as follows:

$$S(y_i) = \frac{e^{y_i}}{\sum_j e^{y_i}}$$

In TensorFlow, the softmax function is implemented. It takes logits and returns softmax activations that have the same type and shape as input logits, as shown in the following image:

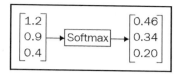

The following code is used to implement this:

```
logit_data = [2.0, 1.0, 0.1]
logits = tf.placeholder(tf.float32)
softmax = tf.nn.softmax(logits)

with tf.Session() as sess:
    output = sess.run(softmax, feed_dict={logits: logit_data})
    print( output )
```

The way we represent labels mathematically is often called **one-hot encoding**. Each label is represented by a vector that has 1.0 for the correct label and 0.0 for everything else. This works well for most problem cases. However, when the problem has millions of labels, one-hot encoding is not efficient, since most of the vector elements are zeros. We measure the similarity distance between two probability vectors, known as **cross-entropy** and denoted by **D**.

Cross-entropy is not symmetric. That means: $D(S,L) \mathrel{!=} D(L,S)$

In machine learning, we define what it means for a model to be bad usually by a mathematical function. This function is called **loss**, **cost**, or **objective** function. One very common function used to determine the loss of a model is called the **cross-entropy loss**. This concept came from information theory (for more on this, please refer to Visual Information Theory at https://colah.github.io/posts/2015-09-Visual-Information/). Intuitively, the loss will be high if the model does a poor job of classifying on the training data, and it will be low otherwise, as shown here:

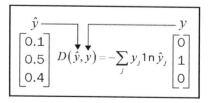

Cross-entropy loss function

In TensorFlow, we can write a cross-entropy function using `tf.reduce_sum()`; it takes an array of numbers and returns its sum as a tensor (see the following code block):

```
x = tf.constant([[1,1,1], [1,1,1]])
with tf.Session() as sess:
    print(sess.run(tf.reduce_sum([1,2,3]))) #returns 6
    print(sess.run(tf.reduce_sum(x,0))) #sum along x axis, prints [2,2,2]
```

But in practice, while computing the softmax function, intermediate terms may be very large due to the exponentials. So, dividing large numbers can be numerically unstable. We should use TensorFlow's provided softmax and cross-entropy loss API. The following code snippet manually calculates cross-entropy loss and also prints the same using the TensorFlow API:

```
import tensorflow as tf

softmax_data = [0.1,0.5,0.4]
onehot_data = [0.0,1.0,0.0]

softmax = tf.placeholder(tf.float32)
onehot_encoding = tf.placeholder(tf.float32)

cross_entropy = -
tf.reduce_sum(tf.multiply(onehot_encoding,tf.log(softmax)))

cross_entropy_loss =
tf.nn.softmax_cross_entropy_with_logits(logits=tf.log(softmax),
labels=onehot_encoding)

with tf.Session() as session:
    print(session.run(cross_entropy,feed_dict={softmax:softmax_data,
onehot_encoding:onehot_data} ))
    print(session.run(cross_entropy_loss,feed_dict={softmax:softmax_data,
onehot_encoding:onehot_data} ))
```

# Introduction to the MNIST dataset

Here we use **MNIST (Modified National Institute of Standards and Technology)**, which consists of images of handwritten numbers and their labels. Since its release in 1999, this classic dataset is used for benchmarking classification algorithms.

The data files `train.csv` and `test.csv` consist of hand-drawn digits, from 0 through 9 in the form of gray-scale images. A digital image is a mathematical function of the form $f(x,y)=pixel$ value. The images are two dimensional.

We can perform any mathematical function on the image. By computing the gradient on the image, we can measure how fast pixel values are changing and the direction in which they are changing. For image recognition, we convert the image into grayscale for simplicity and have one color channel. **RGB** representation of an image consists of three color channels, **RED, BLUE,** and **GREEN**. In the RGB color scheme, an image is a stack of three images RED, BLUE, and GREEN. In a grayscale color scheme, color is not important. Color images are computationally harder to analyze because they take more space in memory. Intensity, which is a measure of the lightness and darkness of an image, is very useful for recognizing objects. In some applications, for example, detecting lane lines in a self-driving car application, color is important because it has to distinguish yellow lanes and white lanes. A grayscale image does not provide enough information to distinguish between white and yellow lane lines.

Any grayscale image is interpreted by the computer as a matrix with one entry for each image pixel. Each image is 28 x 28 pixels in height and width, to give a sum of 784 pixels. Each pixel has a single pixel-value associated with it. This value indicates the lightness or darkness of that particular pixel. This pixel-value is an integer ranging from 0 to 255, where a value of zero means darkest and 255 is the whitest, and a gray pixel is between 0 and 255.

# The simplest artificial neural network

The following image represents a simple two-layer neural network:

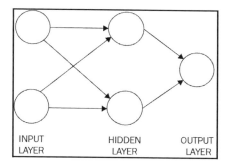

Simple two-layer neural net

The first layer is the **input layer** and the last layer is the **output layer**. The middle layer is the **hidden layer**. If there is more than one hidden layer, then such a network is a deep neural network.

The input and output of each neuron in the hidden layer is connected to each neuron in the next layer. There can be any number of neurons in each layer depending on the problem. Let us consider an example. The simple example which you may already know is the popular hand written digit recognition that detects a number, say 5. This network will accept an image of 5 and will output 1 or 0. A 1 is to indicate the image in fact is a 5 and 0 otherwise. Once the network is created, it has to be trained. We can initialize with random weights and then feed input samples known as the **training dataset**. For each input sample, we check the output, compute the error rate and then adjust the weights so that whenever it sees 5 it outputs 1 and for everything else it outputs a zero. This type of training is called **supervised learning** and the method of adjusting the weights is called **backpropagation**. When constructing artificial neural network models, one of the primary considerations is how to choose activation functions for hidden and output layers. The three most commonly used activation functions are the sigmoid function, hyperbolic tangent function, and **Rectified Linear Unit (ReLU)**. The beauty of the sigmoid function is that its derivative is evaluated at $z$ and is simply $z$ multiplied by 1-minus $z$. That means:

$$dy/dx = \sigma(x)(1-\sigma(x))$$

This helps us to efficiently calculate gradients used in neural networks in a convenient manner. If the feed-forward activations of the logistic function for a given layer is kept in memory, the gradients for that particular layer can be evaluated with the help of simple multiplication and subtraction rather than implementing and re-evaluating the sigmoid function, since it requires extra exponentiation. The following image shows us the ReLU activation function, which is zero when $x < 0$ and then linear with slope 1 when $x > 0$:

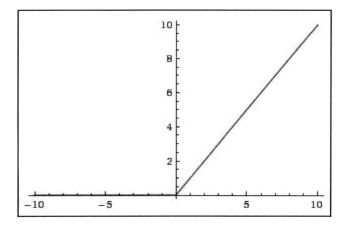

The ReLU is a nonlinear function that computes the function *f(x)=max(0, x)*. That means a ReLU function is 0 for negative inputs and *x* for all inputs *x >0*. This means that the activation is thresholded at zero (see the preceding image on the left). TensorFlow implements the ReLU function in `tf.nn.relu()`:

$$relu(x) = \begin{cases} x \ if \ x >= 0 \\ 0 \ if \ x < 0 \end{cases}$$

*Backpropagation, an abbreviation for "backward propagation of errors", is a common method of training artificial neural networks used in conjunction with an optimization method such as gradient descent. The method calculates the gradient of a loss function with respect to all the weights in the network. The optimization method is fed with the gradient and uses it to get the weights updated to reduce the loss function.*

# Building a single-layer neural network with TensorFlow

Let us build a single-layer neural net with TensorFlow step by step. In this example, we'll be using the MNIST dataset. This dataset is a set of 28 x 28 pixel grayscale images of hand written digits. This dataset consists of 55,000 training data, 10,000 test data, and 5,000 validation data. Every MNIST data point has two parts: an image of a handwritten digit and a corresponding label. The following code block loads data. `one_hot=True` means that the labels are one-hot encoded vectors instead of actual digits of the label. For example, if the label is 2, you will see [0,0,1,0,0,0,0,0,0,0]. This allows us to directly use it in the output layer of the network:

```
from tensorflow.examples.tutorials.mnist import input_data
mnist = input_data.read_data_sets("MNIST_data/", one_hot=True)
```

Setting up placeholders and variables is done as follows:

```
# All the pixels in the image (28 * 28 = 784)
features_count = 784
# there are 10 digits i.e labels
labels_count = 10
batch_size = 128
epochs = 10
learning_rate = 0.5

features = tf.placeholder(tf.float32, [None,features_count])
labels = tf.placeholder(tf.float32, [None, labels_count])

#Set the weights and biases tensors
weights = tf.Variable(tf.truncated_normal((features_count, labels_count)))
biases = tf.Variable(tf.zeros(labels_count),name='biases')
```

Let's set up the optimizer in TensorFlow:

```
loss,
optimizer = tf.train.GradientDescentOptimizer(learning_rate).minimize(loss)
```

Before we begin training, let's set up the variable initialization operation and an operation to measure the accuracy of our predictions, as follows:

```
# Linear Function WX + b
logits = tf.add(tf.matmul(features, weights),biases)

prediction = tf.nn.softmax(logits)

# Cross entropy
cross_entropy = -tf.reduce_sum(labels * tf.log(prediction),
reduction_indices=1)

# Training loss
loss = tf.reduce_mean(cross_entropy)

# Initializing all variables
init = tf.global_variables_initializer()

# Determining if the predictions are accurate
is_correct_prediction = tf.equal(tf.argmax(prediction, 1),
tf.argmax(labels, 1))
# Calculating prediction accuracy
accuracy = tf.reduce_mean(tf.cast(is_correct_prediction, tf.float32))
```

Now we can begin training the model, as shown in the following code snippet:

```
#Beginning the session
with tf.Session() as sess:
    # initializing all the variables
    sess.run(init)
    total_batch = int(len(mnist.train.labels) / batch_size)
    for epoch in range(epochs):
        avg_cost = 0
        for i in range(total_batch):
            batch_x, batch_y =
mnist.train.next_batch(batch_size=batch_size)
            _, c = sess.run([optimizer,loss], feed_dict={features: batch_x,
labels: batch_y})
            avg_cost += c / total_batch
        print("Epoch:", (epoch + 1), "cost =", "{:.3f}".format(avg_cost))
    print(sess.run(accuracy, feed_dict={features: mnist.test.images, labels:
mnist.test.labels}))
```

# Keras deep learning library overview

Keras is a high-level deep neural networks API in Python that runs on top of TensorFlow, CNTK, or Theano.

Here are some core concepts you need to know for working with Keras. TensorFlow is a deep learning library for numerical computation and machine intelligence. It is open source and uses data flow graphs for numerical computation. Mathematical operations are represented by nodes and multidimensional data arrays; that is, tensors are represented by graph edges. This framework is extremely technical and hence it is probably difficult for data analysts. Keras makes deep neural network coding simple. It also runs seamlessly on CPU and GPU machines.

A **model** is the core data structure of Keras. The sequential model, which consists of a linear stack of layers, is the simplest type of model. It provides common functions, such as fit(), evaluate(), and compile().

You can create a sequential model with the help of the following lines of code:

```
from keras.models import Sequential

#Creating the Sequential model
model = Sequential()
```

# Layers in the Keras model

A Keras layer is just like a neural network layer. There are fully connected layers, max pool layers, and activation layers. A layer can be added to the model using the model's `add()` function. For example, a simple model can be represented by the following:

```
from keras.models import Sequential
from keras.layers.core import Dense, Activation, Flatten

#Creating the Sequential model
model = Sequential()

#Layer 1 - Adding a flatten layer
model.add(Flatten(input_shape=(32, 32, 3)))

#Layer 2 - Adding a fully connected layer
model.add(Dense(100))

#Layer 3 - Adding a ReLU activation layer
model.add(Activation('relu'))

#Layer 4- Adding a fully connected layer
model.add(Dense(60))

#Layer 5 - Adding an ReLU activation layer
model.add(Activation('relu'))
```

Keras will automatically infer the shape of all layers after the first layer. This means you only have to set the input dimensions for the first layer. The first layer from the preceding code snippet, `model.add(Flatten(input_shape=(32, 32, 3)))`, sets the input dimension to (32, 32, 3) and the output dimension to (3072=32 x 32 x 3). The second layer takes in the output of the first layer and sets the output dimensions to (100). This chain of passing the output to the next layer continues until the last layer, which is the output of the model.

# Handwritten number recognition with Keras and MNIST

A typical neural network for a digit recognizer may have 784 input pixels connected to 1,000 neurons in the hidden layer, which in turn connects to 10 output targets — one for each digit. Each layer is fully connected to the layer above. A graphical representation of this network is shown as follows, where x are the inputs, h are the hidden neurons, and y are the output class variables:

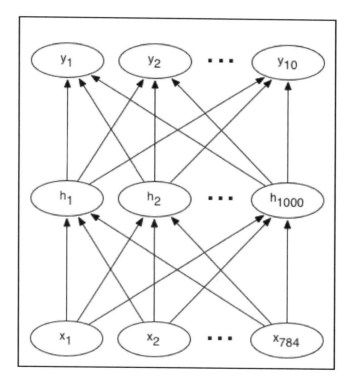

In this notebook, we will build a neural network that will recognize handwritten numbers from 0-9.

The type of neural network that we are building is used in a number of real-world applications, such as recognizing phone numbers and sorting postal mail by address. To build this network, we will use the **MNIST** dataset.

We will begin as shown in the following code by importing all the required modules, after which the data will be loaded, and then finally building the network:

```
# Import Numpy, keras and MNIST data
import numpy as np
import matplotlib.pyplot as plt

from keras.datasets import mnist
from keras.models import Sequential
from keras.layers.core import Dense, Dropout, Activation
from keras.utils import np_utils
```

# Retrieving training and test data

The MNIST dataset already comprises both training and test data. There are 60,000 data points of training data and 10,000 points of test data. If you do not have the data file locally at the `'~/.keras/datasets/'` + path, it can be downloaded at this location.

Each MNIST data point has:

- An image of a handwritten digit
- A corresponding label that is a number from 0-9 to help identify the image

The images will be called, and will be the input to our neural network, **X**; their corresponding labels are **y**.

We want our labels as one-hot vectors. One-hot vectors are vectors of many zeros and one. It's easiest to see this in an example. The number 0 is represented as [1, 0, 0, 0, 0, 0, 0, 0, 0, 0], and 4 is represented as [0, 0, 0, 0, 1, 0, 0, 0, 0, 0] as a one-hot vector.

## Flattened data

We will use flattened data in this example, or a representation of MNIST images in one dimension rather than two can also be used. Thus, each 28 x 28 pixels number image will be represented as a 784 pixel 1 dimensional array.

By flattening the data, information about the 2D structure of the image is thrown; however, our data is simplified. With the help of this, all our training data can be contained in one array of shape (60,000, 784), wherein the first dimension represents the number of training images and the second depicts the number of pixels in each image. This kind of data is easy to analyze using a simple neural network, as follows:

```
# Retrieving the training and test data
(X_train, y_train), (X_test, y_test) = mnist.load_data()


print('X_train shape:', X_train.shape)
print('X_test shape: ', X_test.shape)
print('y_train shape:',y_train.shape)
print('y_test shape: ', y_test.shape)
```

# Visualizing the training data

The following function will help you visualize the MNIST data. By passing in the index of a training example, the show_digit function will display that training image along with its corresponding label in the title:

```
# Visualize the data
import matplotlib.pyplot as plt
%matplotlib inline

#Displaying a training image by its index in the MNIST set
def display_digit(index):
    label = y_train[index].argmax(axis=0)
    image = X_train[index]
    plt.title('Training data, index: %d,  Label: %d' % (index, label))
    plt.imshow(image, cmap='gray_r')
    plt.show()
# Displaying the first (index 0) training image
display_digit(0)

X_train = X_train.reshape(60000, 784)
X_test = X_test.reshape(10000, 784)
X_train = X_train.astype('float32')
X_test = X_test.astype('float32')
X_train /= 255
X_test /= 255
print("Train the matrix shape", X_train.shape)
print("Test the matrix shape", X_test.shape)
```

```
#One Hot encoding of labels.
from keras.utils.np_utils import to_categorical
print(y_train.shape)
y_train = to_categorical(y_train, 10)
y_test = to_categorical(y_test, 10)
print(y_train.shape)
```

# Building the network

For this example, you'll define the following:

- The input layer, which you should expect for each piece of MNIST data, as it tells the network the number of inputs
- Hidden layers, as they recognize patterns in data and also connect the input layer to the output layer
- The output layer, as it defines how the network learns and gives a label as the output for a given image, as follows:

```
# Defining the neural network
def build_model():
    model = Sequential()
    model.add(Dense(512, input_shape=(784,)))
    model.add(Activation('relu')) # An "activation" is just a non-linear
function that is applied to the output
 # of the above layer. In this case, with a "rectified linear unit",
 # we perform clamping on all values below 0 to 0.
    model.add(Dropout(0.2))    #With the help of Dropout helps we can
protect the model from memorizing or "overfitting" the training data
    model.add(Dense(512))
    model.add(Activation('relu'))
    model.add(Dropout(0.2))
    model.add(Dense(10))
    model.add(Activation('softmax')) # This special "softmax" activation,
    #It also ensures that the output is a valid probability distribution,
    #Meaning that values obtained are all non-negative and sum up to 1.
    return model

#Building the model
model = build_model()

model.compile(optimizer='rmsprop',
        loss='categorical_crossentropy',
        metrics=['accuracy'])
```

# Training the network

Now that we've constructed the network, we feed it with data and train it, as follows:

```
# Training
model.fit(X_train, y_train, batch_size=128, nb_epoch=4,
verbose=1,validation_data=(X_test, y_test))
```

# Testing

After you're satisfied with the training output and accuracy, you can run the network on the **test dataset** to measure its performance!

> Keep in mind to perform this only after you've completed the training and are satisfied with the results.

A good result will obtain an accuracy **higher than 95%**. Some simple models have been known to achieve even up to 99.7% accuracy! We can test the model, as shown here:

```
# Comparing the labels predicted by our model with the actual labels

score = model.evaluate(X_test, y_test, batch_size=32,
verbose=1,sample_weight=None)
# Printing the result
print('Test score:', score[0])
print('Test accuracy:', score[1])
```

# Understanding backpropagation

In this section, we will understand an intuition about backpropagation. This is a way of computing gradients using the chain rule. Understanding this process and its subtleties is critical for you to be able to understand and effectively develop, design, and debug neural networks.

In general, given a function *f(x)*, where *x* is a vector of inputs, we want to compute the gradient of *f* at *x* denoted by *V(f(x))*. This is because in the case of neural networks, the function *f* is basically a loss function (*L*) and the input *x* is the combination of weights and training data. The symbol $V$ is pronounced as **nabla**:

$$(xi, yi) \ i = 1......N$$

Why do we take the gradient on weight parameters?

It is given that the training data is usually fixed and the parameters are variables that we have control over. We usually compute the gradient of the parameters so that we can use it for parameter updates. The gradient *Vf* is the vector of partial derivatives, that is:

$$Vf = [\ df/dx, df/dy] = [y,x]$$

In a nutshell, backpropagation will consist of:

- Doing a feed-forward operation
- Comparing the output of the model with the desired output
- Calculating the error
- Running the feedforward operation backwards (backpropagation) to spread the error to each of the weights
- Using this to update the weights, and get a better model
- Continuing this until we have a model that is good

We will be building a neural network that recognizes digits from 0 to 9. This kind of network application is used for sorting postal mail by zip code, recognizing phone numbers and house numbers from images, extracting package quantities from image of the package and so on.

In most cases, backpropagation is implemented in a framework, such as TensorFlow. However, it is not always true that by simply adding an arbitrary number of hidden layers, backpropagation will magically work on the dataset. The fact is if the weight initialization is sloppy, these non linearity functions can saturate and stop learning. That means training loss will be flat and refuse to go down. This is known as the **vanishing gradient problem**.

If your weight matrix *W* is initialized too large, the output of the matrix multiply too could probably have a very large range, which in turn will make all the outputs in the vector *z* almost binary: either 1 or 0. However, if this is the case, then, *z\*(1-z)*, which is the local gradient of the sigmoid non-linearity, will become *zero* (vanish) in both cases, which will make the gradient for both *x* and *W* also zero. The rest of the backward pass will also come out all zero from this point onward on account of the multiplication in the chain rule.

Another nonlinear activation function is ReLU, which thresholds neurons at zero shown as follows. The forward and backward pass for a fully connected layer that uses ReLU would at the core include:

```
z = np.maximum(0, np.dot(W, x)) #Representing forward pass
dW = np.outer(z > 0, x) #Representing backward pass: local gradient for W
```

If you observe this for a while, you'll see that should a neuron get clamped to zero in the forward pass (that is, *z* = 0, it doesn't fire), then its weights will get a zero gradient. This can lead to what is called the **dead ReLU** problem. This means if a ReLU neuron is unfortunately initialized in such a way that it never fires, or if a neuron's weights ever get knocked off with a large update during training into this regime, in such cases this neuron will remain permanently dead. It is similar to permanent, irrecoverable brain damage. Sometimes, you can even forward the entire training set through a trained network and finally realize that a large fraction (about 40%) of your neurons were zero the entire time.

In calculus, the chain rule is used for computing the derivative of the composition of two or more functions. That is, if we have two functions as *f* and *g*, then the chain rule represents the derivative of their composition *f* ∘ *g*. The function that maps *x* to *f(g(x))*) in terms of the derivatives of *f* and *g* and the product of functions is expressed as follows:

$$(f \circ g)' = (f' \circ g) \cdot g'.$$

There is a more explicit way to represent this in terms of the variable. Let *F* = *f* ∘ *g*, or equivalently, *F(x)* = *f(g(x))* for all *x*. Then one can also write:

$$F'(x) = f'(g(x))g'(x).$$

The chain rule can be written with the help of Leibniz's notation in the following way. If a variable *z* is dependent on a variable *y*, which in turn is dependent on a variable *x* (such that *y* and *z* are dependent variables), then *z* depends on *x* as well via the intermediate *y*. The chain rule then states:

$$\frac{dz}{dx} = \frac{dz}{dy} \cdot \frac{dy}{dx}.$$

```
z = 1/(1 + np.exp(-np.dot(W, x))) # forward pass
dx = np.dot(W.T, z*(1-z)) # backward pass: local gradient for x
dW = np.outer(z*(1-z), x) # backward pass: local gradient for W
```

The forward pass on the left in the following figure calculates $z$ as a function $f(x,y)$ using the input variables $x$ and $y$. The right side of the figures represents the backward pass. Receiving $dL/dz$, the gradient of the loss function with respect to $z$, the gradients of $x$ and $y$ on the loss function can be calculated by applying the chain rule, as shown in the following figure:

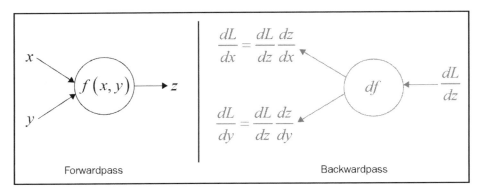

# Summary

In this chapter, we laid the foundation of neural networks and walked through the simplest artificial neural network. We learned how to build a single layer neural network using TensorFlow.

We studied the differences in the layers in the Keras model and demonstrated the famous handwritten number recognition with Keras and MNIST.

Finally, we understood what backpropagation is and used the MNIST dataset to build our network and train and test our data.

In the next chapter, we will introduce you to CNNs.

# 2
# Introduction to Convolutional Neural Networks

**Convolutional Neural Networks** (**CNNs**) are everywhere. In the last five years, we have seen a dramatic rise in the performance of visual recognition systems due to the introduction of deep architectures for feature learning and classification. CNNs have achieved good performance in a variety of areas, such as automatic speech understanding, computer vision, language translation, self-driving cars, and games such as Alpha Go. Thus, the applications of CNNs are almost limitless. DeepMind (from Google) recently published WaveNet, which uses a CNN to generate speech that mimics any human voice (https://deepmind.com/blog/wavenet-generative-model-raw-audio/).

In this chapter, we will cover the following topics:

- History of CNNs
- Overview of a CNN
- Image augmentation

# History of CNNs

There have been numerous attempts to recognize pictures by machines for decades. It is a challenge to mimic the visual recognition system of the human brain in a computer. Human vision is the hardest to mimic and most complex sensory cognitive system of the brain. We will not discuss biological neurons here, that is, the primary visual cortex, but rather focus on artificial neurons. Objects in the physical world are three dimensional, whereas pictures of those objects are two dimensional. In this book, we will introduce neural networks without appealing to brain analogies. In 1963, computer scientist Larry Roberts, who is also known as the **father of computer vision**, described the possibility of extracting 3D geometrical information from 2D perspective views of blocks in his research dissertation titled **BLOCK WORLD**. This was the first breakthrough in the world of computer vision. Many researchers worldwide in machine learning and artificial intelligence followed this work and studied computer vision in the context of BLOCK WORLD. Human beings can recognize blocks regardless of any orientation or lighting changes that may happen. In this dissertation, he said that it is important to understand simple edge-like shapes in images. He extracted these edge-like shapes from blocks in order to make the computer understand that these two blocks are the same irrespective of orientation:

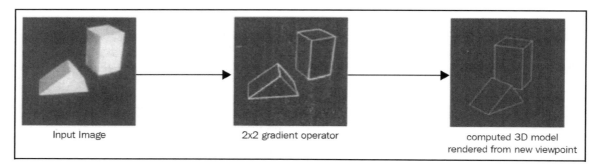

Input Image      2x2 gradient operator      computed 3D model rendered from new viewpoint

The vision starts with a simple structure. This is the beginning of computer vision as an engineering model. David Mark, an MIT computer vision scientist, gave us the next important concept, that vision is hierarchical. He wrote a very influential book named *VISION*. This is a simple book. He said that an image consists of several layers. These two principles form the basis of deep learning architecture, although they do not tell us what kind of mathematical model to use.

In the 1970s, the first visual recognition algorithm, known as the **generalized cylinder model**, came from the AI lab at Stanford University. The idea here is that the world is composed of simple shapes and any real-world object is a combination of these simple shapes. At the same time, another model, known as the **pictorial structure model**, was published from SRI Inc. The concept is still the same as the generalized cylinder model, but the parts are connected by springs; thus, it introduced a concept of variability. The first visual recognition algorithm was used in a digital camera by Fujifilm in 2006.

# Convolutional neural networks

CNNs, or ConvNets, are quite similar to regular neural networks. They are still made up of neurons with weights that can be learned from data. Each neuron receives some inputs and performs a dot product. They still have a loss function on the last fully connected layer. They can still use a nonlinearity function. All of the tips and techniques that we learned from the last chapter are still valid for CNN. As we saw in the previous chapter, a regular neural network receives input data as a single vector and passes through a series of hidden layers. Every hidden layer consists of a set of neurons, wherein every neuron is fully connected to all the other neurons in the previous layer. Within a single layer, each neuron is completely independent and they do not share any connections. The last fully connected layer, also called the **output layer**, contains class scores in the case of an image classification problem. Generally, there are three main layers in a simple ConvNet. They are the **convolution layer**, the **pooling layer**, and the **fully connected layer**. We can see a simple neural network in the following image:

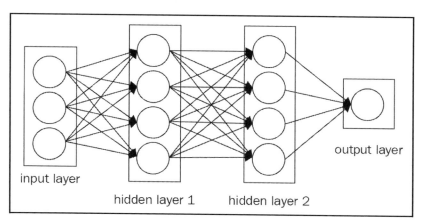

A regular three-layer neural network

So, what changes? Since a CNN mostly takes images as input, this allows us to encode a few properties into the network, thus reducing the number of parameters.

In the case of real-world image data, CNNs perform better than **Multi-Layer Perceptrons (MLPs)**. There are two reasons for this:

- In the last chapter, we saw that in order to feed an image to an MLP, we convert the input matrix into a simple numeric vector with no spatial structure. It has no knowledge that these numbers are spatially arranged. So, CNNs are built for this very reason; that is, to elucidate the patterns in multidimensional data. Unlike MLPs, CNNs understand the fact that image pixels that are closer in proximity to each other are more heavily related than pixels that are further apart:

  *CNN = Input layer + hidden layer + fully connected layer*

- CNNs differ from MLPs in the types of hidden layers that can be included in the model. A ConvNet arranges its neurons in three dimensions: **width**, **height**, and **depth**. Each layer transforms its 3D input volume into a 3D output volume of neurons using activation functions. For example, in the following figure, the red input layer holds the image. Thus its width and height are the dimensions of the image, and the depth is three since there are Red, Green, and Blue channels:

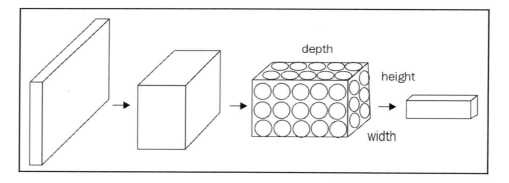

 ConvNets are deep neural networks that share their parameters across space.

# How do computers interpret images?

Essentially, every image can be represented as a matrix of pixel values. In other words, images can be thought of as a function ($f$) that maps from $R^2$ to R.

$f(x, y)$ gives the intensity value at the position $(x, y)$. In practice, the value of the function ranges only from $0$ to $255$. Similarly, a color image can be represented as a stack of three functions. We can write this as a vector of:

$$f( x, y) = [ r(x,y) \ g(x,y) \ b(x,y)]$$

Or we can write this as a mapping:

$$f: R \ x \ R --> R3$$

So, a color image is also a function, but in this case, a value at each $(x,y)$ position is not a single number. Instead it is a vector that has three different light intensities corresponding to three color channels. The following is the code for seeing the details of an image as input to a computer.

# Code for visualizing an image

Let's take a look at how an image can be visualized with the following code:

```
#import all required lib
import matplotlib.pyplot as plt
%matplotlib inline
import numpy as np
from skimage.io import imread
from skimage.transform import resize

# Load a color image in grayscale
image = imread('sample_digit.png',as_grey=True)
image = resize(image,(28,28),mode='reflect')
print('This image is: ',type(image),
        'with dimensions:', image.shape)

plt.imshow(image,cmap='gray')
```

We obtain the following image as a result:

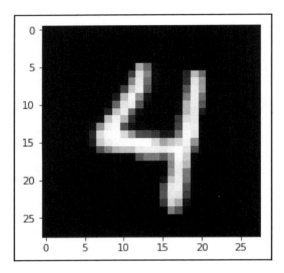

```
def visualize_input(img, ax):

    ax.imshow(img, cmap='gray')
    width, height = img.shape
    thresh = img.max()/2.5
    for x in range(width):
        for y in range(height):
            ax.annotate(str(round(img[x][y],2)), xy=(y,x),
                        horizontalalignment='center',
                        verticalalignment='center',
                        color='white' if img[x][y]<thresh else 'black')

fig = plt.figure(figsize = (12,12))
ax = fig.add_subplot(111)
visualize_input(image, ax)
```

The following result is obtained:

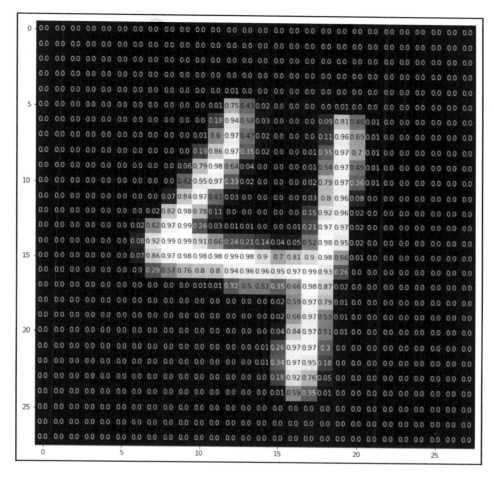

In the previous chapter, we used an MLP-based approach to recognize images. There are two issues with that approach:

- It increases the number of parameters
- It only accepts vectors as input, that is, flattening a matrix to a vector

This means we must find a new way to process images, in which 2D information is not completely lost. CNNs address this issue. Furthermore, CNNs accept matrices as input. Convolutional layers preserve spatial structures. First, we define a convolution window, also called a **filter**, or **kernel**; then slide this over the image.

# Dropout

A neural network can be thought of as a search problem. Each node in the neural network is searching for correlation between the input data and the correct output data.

Dropout randomly turns nodes off while forward-propagating and thus helps ward off weights from converging to identical positions. After this is done, it turns on all the nodes and back-propagates. Similarly, we can set some of the layer's values to zero at random during forward propagation in order to perform dropout on a layer.

 Use dropout only during training. Do not use it at runtime or on your testing dataset.

# Input layer

The **input layer** holds the image data. In the following figure, the input layer consists of three inputs. In a **fully connected layer**, the neurons between two adjacent layers are fully connected pairwise but do not share any connection within a layer. In other words, the neurons in this layer have full connections to all activations in the previous layer. Therefore, their activations can be computed with a simple matrix multiplication, optionally adding a bias term. The difference between a fully connected and convolutional layer is that neurons in a convolutional layer are connected to a local region in the input, and that they also share parameters:

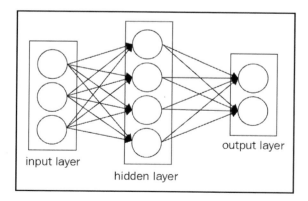

# Convolutional layer

The main objective of convolution in relation to ConvNet is to extract features from the input image. This layer does most of the computation in a ConvNet. We will not go into the mathematical details of convolution here but will get an understanding of how it works over images.

The ReLU activation function is extremely useful in CNNs.

## Convolutional layers in Keras

To create a convolutional layer in Keras, you must first import the required modules as follows:

```
from keras.layers import Conv2D
```

Then, you can create a convolutional layer by using the following format:

```
Conv2D(filters, kernel_size, strides, padding, activation='relu',
input_shape)
```

You must pass the following arguments:

- `filters`: The number of filters.
- `kernel_size`: A number specifying both the height and width of the (square) convolution window. There are also some additional optional arguments that you might like to tune.
- `strides`: The stride of the convolution. If you don't specify anything, this is set to one.
- `padding`: This is either `valid` or `same`. If you don't specify anything, the padding is set to `valid`.
- `activation`: This is typically `relu`. If you don't specify anything, no activation is applied. You are strongly encouraged to add a ReLU activation function to every convolutional layer in your networks.

 It is possible to represent both `kernel_size` and `strides` as either a number or a tuple.

When using your convolutional layer as the first layer (appearing after the input layer) in a model, you must provide an additional `input_shape` argument—`input_shape`. It is a tuple specifying the height, width, and depth (in that order) of the input.

Please make sure that the `input_shape` argument is not included if the convolutional layer is not the first layer in your network.

There are many other tunable arguments that you can set to change the behavior of your convolutional layers:

- **Example 1**: In order to build a CNN with an input layer that accepts images of 200 x 200 pixels in grayscale. In such cases, the next layer would be a convolutional layer of 16 filters with width and height as 2. As we go ahead with the convolution we can set the filter to jump 2 pixels together. Therefore, we can build a convolutional, layer with a filter that doesn't pad the images with zeroes with the following code:

  ```
  Conv2D(filters=16, kernel_size=2, strides=2, activation='relu',
  input_shape=(200, 200, 1))
  ```

- **Example 2**: After we build our CNN model, we can have the next layer in it to be a convolutional layer. This layer will have 32 filters with width and height as 3, which would take the layer that was constructed in the previous example as its input. Here, as we proceed with the convolution, we will set the filter to jump one pixel at a time, such that the convolutional layer will be able to see all the regions of the previous layer too. Such a convolutional layer can be constructed with the help of the following code:

  ```
  Conv2D(filters=32, kernel_size=3, padding='same',
  activation='relu')
  ```

- **Example 3**: You can also construct convolutional layers in Keras of size 2 x 2, with 64 filters and a ReLU activation function. Here, the convolution utilizes a stride of 1 with padding set to `valid` and all other arguments set to their default values. Such a convolutional layer can be built using the following code:

  ```
  Conv2D(64, (2,2), activation='relu')
  ```

# Pooling layer

As we have seen, a convolutional layer is a stack of feature maps, with one feature map for each filter. More filters increase the dimensionality of convolution. Higher dimensionality indicates more parameters. So, the pooling layer controls overfitting by progressively reducing the spatial size of the representation to reduce the number of parameters and computation. The pooling layer often takes the convolutional layer as input. The most commonly used pooling approach is **max pooling**. In addition to max pooling, pooling units can also perform other functions such as **average pooling**. In a CNN, we can control the behavior of the convolutional layer by specifying the size of each filter and the number of filters. To increase the number of nodes in a convolutional layer, we can increase the number of filters, and to increase the size of the pattern, we can increase the size of the filter. There are also a few other hyperparameters that can be tuned. One of them is the stride of the convolution. Stride is the amount by which the filter slides over the image. A stride of 1 moves the filter by 1 pixel horizontally and vertically. Here, the convolution becomes the same as the width and depth of the input image. A stride of 2 makes a convolutional layer of half of the width and height of the image. If the filter extends outside of the image, then we can either ignore these unknown values or replace them with zeros. This is known as **padding**. In Keras, we can set `padding = 'valid'` if it is acceptable to lose a few values. Otherwise, set `padding = 'same'`:

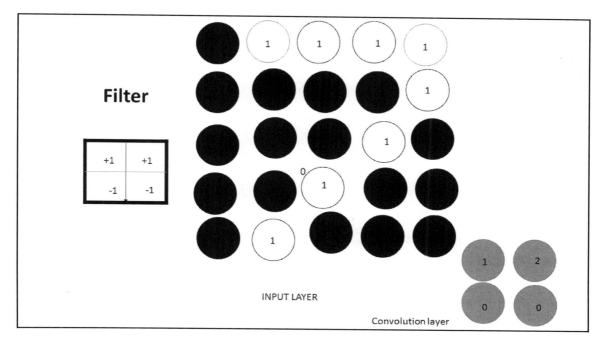

A very simple ConvNet looks like this:

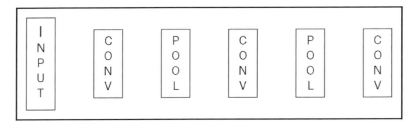

# Practical example – image classification

The convolutional layer helps to detect regional patterns in an image. The max pooling layer, present after the convolutional layer, helps reduce dimensionality. Here is an example of image classification using all the principles we studied in the previous sections. One important notion is to first make all the images into a standard size before doing anything else. The first convolution layer requires an additional `input.shape()` parameter. In this section, we will train a CNN to classify images from the CIFAR-10 database. CIFAR-10 is a dataset of 60,000 color images of 32 x 32 size. These images are labeled into 10 categories with 6,000 images each. These categories are airplane, automobile, bird, cat, dog, deer, frog, horse, ship, and truck. Let's see how to do this with the following code:

```
import keras
import numpy as np
import matplotlib.pyplot as plt
%matplotlib inline

fig = plt.figure(figsize=(20,5))
for i in range(36):
    ax = fig.add_subplot(3, 12, i + 1, xticks=[], yticks=[])
    ax.imshow(np.squeeze(x_train[i]))from keras.datasets import cifar10

# rescale [0,255] --> [0,1]
x_train = x_train.astype('float32')/255
from keras.utils import np_utils

# one-hot encode the labels
num_classes = len(np.unique(y_train))
y_train = keras.utils.to_categorical(y_train, num_classes)
y_test = keras.utils.to_categorical(y_test, num_classes)
```

```
# break training set into training and validation sets
(x_train, x_valid) = x_train[5000:], x_train[:5000]
(y_train, y_valid) = y_train[5000:], y_train[:5000]

# print shape of training set
print('x_train shape:', x_train.shape)

# printing number of training, validation, and test images
print(x_train.shape[0], 'train samples')
print(x_test.shape[0], 'test samples')
print(x_valid.shape[0], 'validation samples')x_test =
x_test.astype('float32')/255


from keras.models import Sequential
from keras.layers import Conv2D, MaxPooling2D, Flatten, Dense, Dropout

model = Sequential()
model.add(Conv2D(filters=16, kernel_size=2, padding='same',
activation='relu',
                          input_shape=(32, 32, 3)))
model.add(MaxPooling2D(pool_size=2))
model.add(Conv2D(filters=32, kernel_size=2, padding='same',
activation='relu'))
model.add(MaxPooling2D(pool_size=2))
model.add(Conv2D(filters=64, kernel_size=2, padding='same',
activation='relu'))
model.add(MaxPooling2D(pool_size=2))
model.add(Conv2D(filters=32, kernel_size=2, padding='same',
activation='relu'))
model.add(MaxPooling2D(pool_size=2))
model.add(Dropout(0.3))
model.add(Flatten())
model.add(Dense(500, activation='relu'))
model.add(Dropout(0.4))
model.add(Dense(10, activation='softmax'))

model.summary()

# compile the model
model.compile(loss='categorical_crossentropy', optimizer='rmsprop',
                metrics=['accuracy'])
from keras.callbacks import ModelCheckpoint

# train the model
checkpointer = ModelCheckpoint(filepath='model.weights.best.hdf5',
verbose=1,
                                  save_best_only=True)
```

```
hist = model.fit(x_train, y_train, batch_size=32, epochs=100,
        validation_data=(x_valid, y_valid), callbacks=[checkpointer],
        verbose=2, shuffle=True)
```

# Image augmentation

While training a CNN model, we do not want the model to change any prediction based on the size, angle, and position of the image. The image is represented as a matrix of pixel values, so the size, angle, and position have a huge effect on the pixel values. To make the model more size-invariant, we can add different sizes of the image to the training set. Similarly, in order to make the model more rotation-invariant, we can add images with different angles. This process is known as **image data augmentation**. This also helps to avoid overfitting. Overfitting happens when a model is exposed to very few samples. Image data augmentation is one way to reduce overfitting, but it may not be enough because augmented images are still correlated. Keras provides an image augmentation class called `ImageDataGenerator` that defines the configuration for image data augmentation. This also provides other features such as:

- Sample-wise and feature-wise standardization
- Random rotation, shifts, shear, and zoom of the image
- Horizontal and vertical flip
- ZCA whitening
- Dimension reordering
- Saving the changes to disk

An augmented image generator object can be created as follows:

```
imagedatagen = ImageDataGenerator()
```

This API generates batches of tensor image data in real-time data augmentation, instead of processing an entire image dataset in memory. This API is designed to create augmented image data during the model fitting process. Thus, it reduces the memory overhead but adds some time cost for model training.

After it is created and configured, you must fit your data. This computes any statistics required to perform the transformations to image data. This is done by calling the `fit()` function on the data generator and passing it to the training dataset, as follows:

```
imagedatagen.fit(train_data)
```

The batch size can be configured, the data generator can be prepared, and batches of images can be received by calling the `flow()` function:

```
imagedatagen.flow(x_train, y_train, batch_size=32)
```

Finally, call the `fit_generator()` function instead of calling the `fit()` function on the model:

```
fit_generator(imagedatagen, samples_per_epoch=len(X_train), epochs=200)
```

Let's look at some examples to understand how the image augmentation API in Keras works. We will use the MNIST handwritten digit recognition task in these examples.

Let's begin by taking a look at the first nine images in the training dataset:

```
#Plot images
from keras.datasets import mnist
from matplotlib import pyplot
#loading data
(X_train, y_train), (X_test, y_test) = mnist.load_data()
#creating a grid of 3x3 images
for i in range(0, 9):
  pyplot.subplot(330 + 1 + i)
  pyplot.imshow(X_train[i], cmap=pyplot.get_cmap('gray'))
#Displaying the plot
pyplot.show()
```

The following code snippet creates augmented images from the CIFAR-10 dataset. We will add these images to the training set of the last example and see how the classification accuracy increases:

```
from keras.preprocessing.image import ImageDataGenerator
# creating and configuring augmented image generator
datagen_train = ImageDataGenerator(
 width_shift_range=0.1, # shifting randomly images horizontally (10% of
total width)
 height_shift_range=0.1, # shifting randomly images vertically (10% of
total height)
 horizontal_flip=True) # flipping randomly images horizontally
# creating and configuring augmented image generator
```

```
datagen_valid = ImageDataGenerator(
  width_shift_range=0.1, # shifting randomly images horizontally (10% of
total width)
  height_shift_range=0.1, # shifting randomly images vertically (10% of
total height)
  horizontal_flip=True) # flipping randomly images horizontally
# fitting augmented image generator on data
datagen_train.fit(x_train)
datagen_valid.fit(x_valid)
```

# Summary

We began this chapter by briefly looking into the history of CNNs. We introduced you to the implementation of visualizing images.

We studied image classification with the help of a practical example, using all the principles we learned about in the chapter. Finally, we learned how image augmentation helps us avoid overfitting and studied the various other features provided by image augmentation.

In the next chapter, we will learn how to build a simple image classifier CNN model from scratch.

# 3
# Build Your First CNN and Performance Optimization

A **convolutional neural network (CNN)** is a type of **feed-forward neural network (FNN)** in which the connectivity pattern between its neurons is inspired by an animal's visual cortex. In the last few years, CNNs have demonstrated superhuman performance in image search services, self-driving cars, automatic video classification, voice recognition, and **natural language processing (NLP)**.

Considering these motivations, in this chapter, we will construct a simple CNN model for image classification from scratch, followed by some theoretical aspects, such as convolutional and pooling operations. Then we will discuss how to tune hyperparameters and optimize the training time of CNNs for improved classification accuracy. Finally, we will build the second CNN model by considering some best practices. In a nutshell, the following topics will be covered in this chapter:

- CNN architectures and drawbacks of DNNs
- The convolution operations and pooling layers
- Creating and training a CNN for image classification
- Model performance optimization
- Creating an improved CNN for optimized performance

# CNN architectures and drawbacks of DNNs

In Chapter 2, *Introduction to Convolutional Neural Networks*, we discussed that a regular multilayer perceptron works fine for small images (for example, MNIST or CIFAR-10). However, it breaks down for larger images because of the huge number of parameters it requires. For example, a 100 × 100 image has 10,000 pixels, and if the first layer has just 1,000 neurons (which already severely restricts the amount of information transmitted to the next layer), this means 10 million connections; and that is just for the first layer.

CNNs solve this problem using partially connected layers. Because consecutive layers are only partially connected and because it heavily reuses its weights, a CNN has far fewer parameters than a fully connected DNN, which makes it much faster to train, reduces the risk of overfitting, and requires much less training data. Moreover, when a CNN has learned a kernel that can detect a particular feature, it can detect that feature anywhere on the image. In contrast, when a DNN learns a feature in one location, it can detect it only in that particular location.

Since images typically have very repetitive features, CNNs are able to generalize much better than DNNs for image processing tasks such as classification, using fewer training examples. Importantly, a DNN has no prior knowledge of how pixels are organized; it does not know that nearby pixels are close. A CNN's architecture embeds this prior knowledge. Lower layers typically identify features in small areas of the images, while higher layers combine the lower-level features into larger features. This works well with most natural images, giving CNNs a decisive head start compared to DNNs:

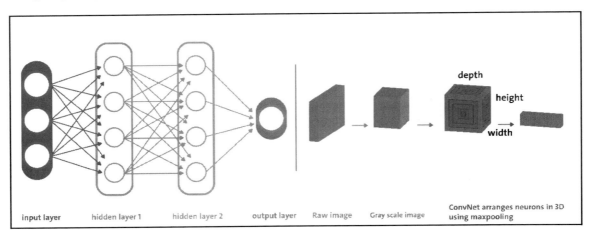

Figure 1: Regular DNN versus CNN, where each layer has neurons arranged in 3D

For example, in *Figure 1*, on the left, you can see a regular three-layer neural network. On the right, a ConvNet arranges its neurons in three dimensions (width, height, and depth) as visualized in one of the layers. Every layer of a ConvNet transforms the 3D input volume to a 3D output volume of neuron activations. The red input layer holds the image, so its width and height would be the dimensions of the image, and the depth would be three (red, green, and blue channels). Therefore, all the multilayer neural networks we looked at had layers composed of a long line of neurons, and we had to flatten input images or data to 1D before feeding them to the neural network.

However, what happens once you try to feed them a 2D image directly? The answer is that in CNNs, each layer is represented in 2D, which makes it easier to match neurons with their corresponding inputs. We will see examples of this in upcoming sections. Another important fact is that all the neurons in a feature map share the same parameters, so it dramatically reduces the number of parameters in the model; but more importantly, it means that once the CNN has learned to recognize a pattern in one location, it can recognize it in any other location.

In contrast, once a regular DNN has learned to recognize a pattern in one location, it can recognize it only in that particular location. In multilayer networks such as MLP or DBN, the outputs of all neurons of the input layer are connected to each neuron in the hidden layer, and then the output will again act as the input to the fully connected layer. In CNN networks, the connection scheme that defines the convolutional layer is significantly different. The convolutional layer is the main type of layer in a CNN, where each neuron is connected to a certain region of the input area called the **receptive field**.

In a typical CNN architecture, a few convolutional layers are connected in a cascade style. Each layer is followed by a **Rectified Linear Unit (ReLU)** layer, then a pooling layer, then one or more convolutional layers (+ReLU), then another pooling layer, and finally one or more fully connected layers. Pretty much depending on problem type, the network might be deep though. The output from each convolution layer is a set of objects called **feature maps**, generated by a single kernel filter. Then the feature maps can be used to define a new input to the next layer.

Each neuron in a CNN network produces an output, followed by an activation threshold, which is proportional to the input and not bound:

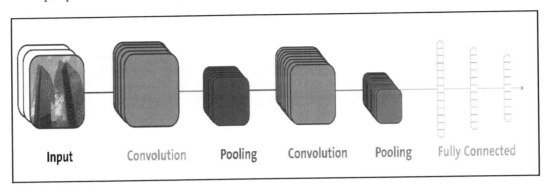

Figure 2: A conceptual architecture of a CNN

As you can see in *Figure 2*, the pooling layers are usually placed after the convolutional layers (for example, between two convolutional layers). A pooling layer into subregions then divides the convolutional region. Then, a single representative value is selected, using either a max-pooling or an average pooling technique, to reduce the computational time of subsequent layers. This way, a CNN can be thought of as a feature extractor. To understand this more clearly, refer to the following figure:

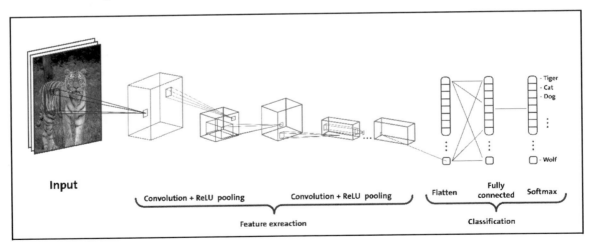

In this way, the robustness of the feature with respect to its spatial position is increased too. To be more specific, when feature maps are used as image properties and pass through the grayscale image, it gets smaller and smaller as it progresses through the network; but it also typically gets deeper and deeper, as more feature maps will be added.

We've already discussed the limitations of such FFNN - that is, a very high number of neurons would be necessary, even in a shallow architecture, due to the very large input sizes associated with images, where each pixel is a relevant variable. The convolution operation brings a solution to this problem as it reduces the number of free parameters, allowing the network to be deeper with fewer parameters.

# Convolutional operations

A convolution is a mathematical operation that slides one function over another and measures the integral of their pointwise multiplication. It has deep connections with the Fourier transformation and the Laplace transformation and is heavily used in signal processing. Convolutional layers actually use cross-correlations, which are very similar to convolutions.

 In mathematics, convolution is a mathematical operation on two functions that produces a third function—that is, the modified (convoluted) version of one of the original functions. The resulting function gives in integral of the pointwise multiplication of the two functions as a function of the amount that one of the original functions is translated. Interested readers can refer to this URL for more information: `https://en.wikipedia.org/wiki/Convolution`.

Thus, the most important building block of a CNN is the convolutional layer. Neurons in the first convolutional layer are not connected to every single pixel in the input image (that is, like FNNs—for example, MLP and DBN) but only to pixels in their receptive fields. See *Figure 3*. In turn, each neuron in the second convolutional layer is connected only to neurons located within a small rectangle in the first layer:

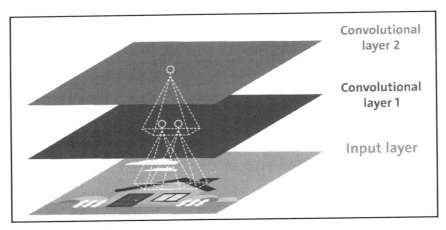

Figure 3: Each convolutional neuron processes data only for its receptive field

In Chapter 2, *Introduction to Convolutional Neural Networks*, we have seen that all multilayer neural networks (for example, MLP) have layers composed of so many neurons, and we have to flatten input images to 1D before feeding them to the neural network. Instead, in a CNN, each layer is represented in 2D, which makes it easier to match neurons with their corresponding inputs.

 The receptive fields concept is used by CNNs to exploit spatial locality by enforcing a local connectivity pattern between neurons of adjacent layers.

This architecture allows the network to concentrate on low-level features in the first hidden layer, and then assemble them into higher-level features in the next hidden layer, and so on. This hierarchical structure is common in real-world images, which is one of the reasons why CNNs work so well for image recognition.

Finally, it not only requires a low number of neurons but also reduces the number of trainable parameters significantly. For example, regardless of image size, building regions of size 5 x 5, each with the same-shared weights, requires only 25 learnable parameters. In this way, it resolves the vanishing or exploding gradients problem in training traditional multilayer neural networks with many layers by using backpropagation.

# Pooling, stride, and padding operations

Once you've understood how convolutional layers work, the pooling layers are quite easy to grasp. A pooling layer typically works on every input channel independently, so the output depth is the same as the input depth. You may alternatively pool over the depth dimension, as we will see next, in which case the image's spatial dimensions (for example, height and width) remain unchanged but the number of channels is reduced. Let's see a formal definition of pooling layers from the well-known TensorFlow website:

> *"The pooling ops sweep a rectangular window over the input tensor, computing a reduction operation for each window (average, max, or max with argmax). Each pooling op uses rectangular windows of size called ksize separated by offset strides. For example, if strides are all ones, every window is used, if strides are all twos, every other window is used in each dimension, and so on."*

Therefore, in summary, just like convolutional layers, each neuron in a pooling layer is connected to the outputs of a limited number of neurons in the previous layer, located within a small rectangular receptive field. However, we must define its size, the stride, and the padding type. So in summary, the output can be computed as follows:

```
output[i] = reduce(value[strides * i:strides * i + ksize]),
```

Here, the indices also take the padding values into consideration.

 A pooling neuron has no weights. Therefore, all it does is aggregate the inputs using an aggregation function such as max or mean.

In other words, the goal of using pooling is to subsample the input image in order to reduce the computational load, memory usage, and number of parameters. This helps to avoid overfitting in the training stage. Reducing the input image size also makes the neural network tolerate a little bit of image shift. The spatial semantics of the convolution ops depend on the padding scheme chosen.

Padding is an operation to increase the size of the input data. In the case of one-dimensional data, you just append/prepend the array with a constant; in two-dimensional data, you surround the matrix with these constants. In n-dimensional, you surround your n-dimensional hypercube with the constant. In most of the cases, this constant is zero and it is called **zero padding**:

- **VALID padding**: Only drops the rightmost columns (or bottommost rows)
- **SAME padding**: Tries to pad evenly left and right, but if the number of columns to be added is odd, it will add the extra column to the right, as is the case in this example

Let's explain the preceding definition graphically, in the following figure. If we want a layer to have the same height and width as the previous layer, it is common to add zeros around the inputs, as shown in the diagram. This is called **SAME** or **zero padding**.

> The term **SAME** means that the output feature map has the same spatial dimensions as the input feature map.

On the other hand, zero padding is introduced to make the shapes match as needed, equally on every side of the input map. **VALID** means no padding and only drops the rightmost columns (or bottommost rows):

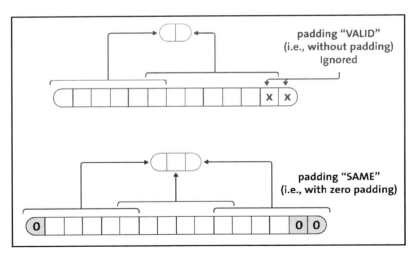

Figure 4: SAME versus VALID padding with CNN

In the following example (*Figure 5*), we use a 2 × 2 pooling kernel and a stride of 2 with no padding. Only the **max** input value in each kernel makes it to the next layer since the other inputs are dropped (we will see this later on):

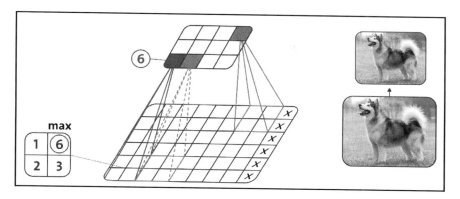

Figure 5: An example using max pooling, that is, subsampling

## Fully connected layer

At the top of the stack, a regular fully connected layer (also known as **FNN** or **dense layer**) is added; it acts similar to an MLP, which might be composed of a few fully connected layers (+ReLUs). The final layer outputs (for example, softmax) the prediction. An example is a softmax layer that outputs estimated class probabilities for a multiclass classification.

Fully connected layers connect every neuron in one layer to every neuron in another layer. Although fully connected FNNs can be used to learn features as well as classify data, it is not practical to apply this architecture to images.

# Convolution and pooling operations in TensorFlow

Now that we have seen how convolutional and pooling operations are performed theoretically, let's see how we can perform these operation hands-on using TensorFlow. So let's get started.

# Applying pooling operations in TensorFlow

Using TensorFlow, a subsampling layer can normally be represented by a `max_pool` operation by maintaining the initial parameters of the layer. For `max_pool`, it has the following signature in TensorFlow:

```
tf.nn.max_pool(value, ksize, strides, padding, data_format, name)
```

Now let's learn how to create a function that utilizes the preceding signature and returns a tensor with type `tf.float32`, that is, the max pooled output tensor:

```
import tensorflow as tf

def maxpool2d(x, k=2):
    return tf.nn.max_pool(x,
            ksize=[1, k, k, 1],
            strides=[1, k, k, 1],
            padding='SAME')
```

In the preceding code segment, the parameters can be described as follows:

- `value`: This is a 4D tensor of `float32` elements and shape (batch length, height, width, and channels)
- `ksize`: A list of integers representing the window size on each dimension
- `strides`: The step of the moving windows on each dimension
- `data_format`: NHWC, NCHW, and NCHW_VECT_C are supported
- `ordering`: NHWC or NCHW
- `padding`: VALID or SAME

However, depending upon the layering structures in a CNN, there are other pooling operations supported by TensorFlow, as follows:

- `tf.nn.avg_pool`: This returns a reduced tensor with the average of each window
- `tf.nn.max_pool_with_argmax`: This returns the `max_pool` tensor and a tensor with the flattened index of `max_value`
- `tf.nn.avg_pool3d`: This performs an `avg_pool` operation with a cubic-like
- window; the input has an added depth
- `tf.nn.max_pool3d`: This performs the same function as (...) but applies the max operation

Now let's see a concrete example of how the padding thing works in TensorFlow. Suppose we have an input image x with shape `[2, 3]` and one channel. Now we want to see the effect of both `VALID` and `SAME` paddings:

- `valid_pad`: Max pool with 2 x 2 kernel, stride 2, and `VALID` padding
- `same_pad`: Max pool with 2 x 2 kernel, stride 2, and `SAME` padding

Let's see how we can attain this in Python and TensorFlow. Suppose we have an input image of shape `[2, 4]`, which is one channel:

```
import tensorflow as tf
x = tf.constant([[2., 4., 6., 8.,],
                 [10., 12., 14., 16.]])
```

Now let's give it a shape accepted by `tf.nn.max_pool`:

```
x = tf.reshape(x, [1, 2, 4, 1])
```

If we want to apply the `VALID` padding with the max pool with a 2 x 2 kernel, stride 2:

```
VALID = tf.nn.max_pool(x, [1, 2, 2, 1], [1, 2, 2, 1], padding='VALID')
```

On the other hand, using the max pool with a 2 x 2 kernel, stride 2 and `SAME` padding:

```
SAME = tf.nn.max_pool(x, [1, 2, 2, 1], [1, 2, 2, 1], padding='SAME')
```

For `VALID` padding, since there is no padding, the output shape is `[1, 1]`. However, for the `SAME` padding, since we pad the image to the shape `[2, 4]` (with `-inf`) and then apply the max pool, the output shape is `[1, 2]`. Let's validate them:

```
print(VALID.get_shape())
print(SAME.get_shape())

>>>
(1, 1, 2, 1)
(1, 1, 2, 1)
```

# Convolution operations in TensorFlow

TensorFlow provides a variety of methods for convolution. The canonical form is applied by the `conv2d` operation. Let's have a look at the usage of this operation:

```
conv2d(
    input,
    filter,
    strides,
    padding,
    use_cudnn_on_gpu=True,
    data_format='NHWC',
    dilations=[1, 1, 1, 1],
    name=None
)
```

The parameters we use are as follows:

- `input`: The operation will be applied to this original tensor. It has a definite format of four dimensions, and the default dimension order is shown next.
- `filter`: This is a tensor representing a kernel or filter. It has a very generic method: (`filter_height`, `filter_width`, `in_channels`, and `out_channels`).
- `strides`: This is a list of four `int` tensor datatypes, which indicate the sliding windows for each dimension.
- `padding`: This can be SAME or VALID. SAME will try to conserve the initial tensor dimension, but VALID will allow it to grow if the output size and padding are computed. We will see later how to perform padding along with the pooling layers.
- `use_cudnn_on_gpu`: This indicates whether to use the CUDA GPU CNN library to accelerate calculations.
- `data_format`: This specifies the order in which data is organized (NHWC or NCWH).
- `dilations`: This signifies an optional list of `ints`. It defaults to (1, 1, 1, 1). 1D tensor of length 4. The dilation factor for each dimension of input. If it is set to k > 1, there will be k-1 skipped cells between each filter element on that dimension. The dimension order is determined by the value of `data_format`; see the preceding code example for details. Dilations in the batch and depth dimensions must be 1.
- `name`: A name for the operation (optional).

The following is an example of a convolutional layer. It concatenates a convolution, adds a bias parameter sum, and finally returns the activation function we have chosen for the whole layer (in this case, the ReLU operation, which is a frequently used one):

```
def conv_layer(data, weights, bias, strides=1):
    x = tf.nn.conv2d(x,
                weights,
                strides=[1, strides, strides, 1],
                padding='SAME')
    x = tf.nn.bias_add(x, bias)
    return tf.nn.relu(x)
```

Here, x is the 4D tensor input (batch size, height, width, and channel). TensorFlow also offers a few other kinds of convolutional layers. For example:

- `tf.layers.conv1d()` creates a convolutional layer for 1D inputs. This is useful, for example, in NLP, where a sentence may be represented as a 1D array of words, and the receptive field covers a few neighboring words.
- `tf.layers.conv3d()` creates a convolutional layer for 3D inputs.
- `tf.nn.atrous_conv2d()` creates an a trous convolutional layer (*a trous* is French for with holes). This is equivalent to using a regular convolutional layer with a filter dilated by inserting rows and columns of zeros. For example, a $1 \times 3$ filter equal to (1, 2, 3) may be dilated with a dilation rate of 4, resulting in a dilated filter (1, 0, 0, 0, 2, 0, 0, 0, 3). This allows the convolutional layer to have a larger receptive field at no computational price and using no extra parameters.
- `tf.layers.conv2d_transpose ()` creates a transpose convolutional layer, sometimes called a **deconvolutional layer,** which up-samples an image. It does so by inserting zeros between the inputs, so you can think of this as a regular convolutional layer using a fractional stride.
- `tf.nn.depthwise_conv2d()` creates a depth-wise convolutional layer that applies every filter to every individual input channel independently. Thus, if there are $f_n$ filters and $f_{n'}$ input channels, then this will output $f_n \times f_{n'}$ feature maps.
- `tf.layers.separable_conv2d()` creates a separable convolutional layer that first acts like a depth-wise convolutional layer and then applies a $1 \times 1$ convolutional layer to the resulting feature maps. This makes it possible to apply filters to arbitrary sets of inputs channels.

# Training a CNN

In the previous section, we have seen how to construct a CNN and apply different operations on its different layers. Now when it comes to training a CNN, it is much trickier as it needs a lot of considerations to control those operations such as applying appropriate activation function, weight and bias initialization, and of course, using optimizers intelligently.

There are also some advanced considerations such as hyperparameter tuning for optimized too. However, that will be discussed in the next section. We first start our discussion with weight and bias initialization.

# Weight and bias initialization

One of the most common initialization techniques in training a DNN is random initialization. The idea of using random initialization is just sampling each weight from a normal distribution of the input dataset with low deviation. Well, a low deviation allows you to bias the network towards the simple 0 solutions.

But what does it mean? The thing is that, the initialization can be completed without the bad repercussions of actually initializing the weights to 0. Secondly, Xavier initialization is often used to train CNNs. It is similar to random initialization but often turns out to work much better. Now let me explain the reason for this:

- Imagine that you initialize the network weights randomly but they turn out to start too small. Then the signal shrinks as it passes through each layer until it is too tiny to be useful.
- On the other hand, if the weights in a network start too large, then the signal grows as it passes through each layer until it is too massive to be useful.

The good thing is that using Xavier initialization makes sure the weights are just right, keeping the signal in a reasonable range of values through many layers. In summary, it can automatically determine the scale of initialization based on the number of input and output neurons.

Interested readers should refer to this publication for detailed information: Xavier Glorot and Yoshua Bengio, *Understanding the difficulty of training deep FNNs*, Proceedings of the 13th International Conference on **Artificial Intelligence and Statistics** (**AISTATS**) 2010, Chia Laguna Resort, Sardinia, Italy. Volume 9 of JMLR: W&CP.

Finally, you may ask an intelligent question, *Can't I get rid of the random initialization while training a regular DNN (for example, MLP or DBN)*? Well, recently, some researchers have been talking about random orthogonal matrix initializations that perform better than just any random initialization for training DNNs:

- **When it comes to initializing the biases**, it is possible and common to initialize the biases to be zero since the asymmetry breaking is provided by the small random numbers in the weights. Setting the biases to a small constant value such as 0.01 for all biases ensures that all ReLU units can propagate some gradient. However, it neither performs well nor does consistent improvement. Therefore, sticking with zero is recommended.

# Regularization

There are several ways of controlling training of CNNs to prevent overfitting in the training phase. For example, L2/L1 regularization, max norm constraints, and drop out:

- **L2 regularization**: This is perhaps the most common form of regularization. It can be implemented by penalizing the squared magnitude of all parameters directly in the objective. For example, using the gradient descent parameter update, L2 regularization ultimately means that every weight is decayed linearly: $W$ += - lambda * $W$ towards zero.

- **L1 regularization**: This is another relatively common form of regularization, where for each weight $w$ we add the term $\lambda|w|$ to the objective. However, it is also possible to possible to combine the L1 regularization with the L2 regularization: $\lambda 1|w|+\lambda 2 w2$, which is commonly known as **Elastic-net regularization**.

- **Max-norm constraints**: Another form of regularization is to enforce an absolute upper bound on the magnitude of the weight vector for every neuron and use projected gradient descent to enforce the constraint.

Finally, dropout is an advanced variant of regularization, which will be discussed later in this chapter.

# Activation functions

The activation ops provide different types of nonlinearities for use in neural networks. These include smooth nonlinearities, such as `sigmoid`, `tanh`, `elu`, `softplus`, and `softsign`. On the other hand, some continuous but not-everywhere-differentiable functions that can be used are `relu`, `relu6`, `crelu`, and `relu_x`. All activation ops apply component-wise and produce a tensor of the same shape as the input tensor. Now let us see how to use a few commonly used activation functions in TensorFlow syntax.

## Using sigmoid

In TensorFlow, the signature `tf.sigmoid(x, name=None)` computes sigmoid of $x$ element-wise using $y = 1 / (1 + exp(-x))$ and returns a tensor with the same type $x$. Here is the parameter description:

- x: A tensor. This must be one of the following types: `float32`, `float64`, `int32`, `complex64`, `int64`, or `qint32`.
- name: A name for the operation (optional).

## Using tanh

In TensorFlow, the signature `tf.tanh(x, name=None)` computes a hyperbolic tangent of $x$ element-wise and returns a tensor with the same type $x$. Here is the parameter description:

- x: A tensor or sparse. This is a tensor with type `float`, `double`, `int32`, `complex64`, `int64`, or `qint32`.
- name: A name for the operation (optional).

## Using ReLU

In TensorFlow, the signature `tf.nn.relu(features, name=None)` computes a rectified linear using `max(features, 0)` and returns a tensor having the same type as features. Here is the parameter description:

- features: A tensor. This must be one of the following types: `float32`, `float64`, `int32`, `int64`, `uint8`, `int16`, `int8`, `uint16`, and `half`.
- name: A name for the operation (optional).

For more on how to use other activation functions, please refer to the TensorFlow website. Up to this point, we have the minimal theoretical knowledge to build our first CNN network for making a prediction.

# Building, training, and evaluating our first CNN

In the next section, we will look at how to classify and distinguish between dogs from cats based on their raw images. We will also look at how to implement our first CNN model to deal with the raw and color image having three channels. This network design and implementation are not straightforward; TensorFlow low-level APIs will be used for this. However, do not worry; later in this chapter, we will see another example of implementing a CNN using TensorFlow's high-level contrib API. Before we formally start, a short description of the dataset is a mandate.

# Dataset description

For this example, we will use the dog versus cat dataset from Kaggle that was provided for the infamous Dogs versus Cats classification problem as a playground competition with kernels enabled. The dataset can be downloaded from `https://www.kaggle.com/c/dogs-vs-cats-redux-kernels-edition/data`.

The train folder contains 25,000 images of dogs and cats. Each image in this folder has the label as part of the filename. The test folder contains 12,500 images, named according to a numeric ID. For each image in the test set, you should predict a probability that the image is a dog (1 = dog, 0 = cat); that is, a binary classification problem. For this example, there are three Python scripts.

# Step 1 – Loading the required packages

Here we import the required packages and libraries. Note that depending upon the platform, your imports might be different:

```
import time
import math
import random
import os
import pandas as pd
```

```
import numpy as np
import matplotlib.pyplot as plt
import tensorflow as tf
import Preprocessor
import cv2
import LayersConstructor
from sklearn.metrics import confusion_matrix
from datetime import timedelta
from sklearn.metrics.classification import accuracy_score
from sklearn.metrics import precision_recall_fscore_support
```

# Step 2 – Loading the training/test images to generate train/test set

We set the number of color channels as 3 for the images. In the previous section, we have seen that it should be 1 for grayscale images:

```
num_channels = 3
```

For the simplicity, we assume the image dimensions should be squares only. Let's set the size to be `128`:

```
img_size = 128
```

Now that we have the image size (that is, `128`) and the number of the channel (that is, 3), the size of the image when flattened to a single dimension would be the multiplication of the image dimension and the number of channels, as follows:

```
img_size_flat = img_size * img_size * num_channels
```

Note that, at a later stage, we might need to reshape the image for the max pooling and convolutional layers, so we need to reshape the image. For our case, it would be the tuple with height and width of images used to reshape arrays:

```
img_shape = (img_size, img_size)
```

We should have explicitly defined the labels (that is, classes) since we only have the raw color image, and so the images do not have the labels like other numeric machine learning dataset, have. Let's explicitly define the class info as follows:

```
classes = ['dogs', 'cats']
num_classes = len(classes)
```

We need to define the batch size that needs to be trained on our CNN model later on:

```
batch_size = 14
```

Note that we also can define what portion of the training set will be used as the validation split. Let's assume that 16% will be used, for simplicity:

```
validation_size = 0.16
```

One important thing to set is how long to wait after the validation loss stops improving before terminating the training. We should use none if we do not want to implement early stopping:

```
early_stopping = None
```

Now, download the dataset and you have to do one thing manually: separate the images of dogs and cats and place them in two separate folders. To be more specific, suppose you put your training set under the path /home/DoG_CaT/data/train/. In the train folder, create two separate folders dogs and cats but only show the path to DoG_CaT/data/train/. We also assume that our test set is in the /home/DoG_CaT/data/test/ directory. In addition, you can define the checkpoint directory where the logs and model checkpoint files will be written:

```
train_path = '/home/DoG_CaT/data/train/'
test_path = '/home/DoG_CaT/data/test/'
checkpoint_dir = "models/"
```

Then we start reading the training set and prepare it for the CNN model. For processing the test and train set, we have another script Preprocessor.py. Nonetheless, it would be better to prepare the test set as well:

```
data = Preprocessor.read_train_sets(train_path, img_size, classes,
validation_size=validation_size)
```

The preceding line of code reads the raw images of cats and dogs and creates the training set. The read_train_sets() function goes as follows:

```
def read_train_sets(train_path, image_size, classes, validation_size=0):
  class DataSets(object):
      pass
      data_sets = DataSets()
      images, labels, ids, cls = load_train(train_path, image_size,
classes)
      images, labels, ids, cls = shuffle(images, labels, ids, cls)
      if isinstance(validation_size, float):
          validation_size = int(validation_size * images.shape[0])
```

```
            validation_images = images[:validation_size]
            validation_labels = labels[:validation_size]
            validation_ids = ids[:validation_size]
            validation_cls = cls[:validation_size]
            train_images = images[validation_size:]
            train_labels = labels[validation_size:]
            train_ids = ids[validation_size:]
            train_cls = cls[validation_size:]
            data_sets.train = DataSet(train_images, train_labels, train_ids,
    train_cls)
            data_sets.valid = DataSet(validation_images, validation_labels,
    validation_ids, validation_cls)
        return data_sets
```

In the previous code segment, we have used the method `load_train()` to load the images which is an instance of a class called `DataSet`:

```
def load_train(train_path, image_size, classes):
    images = []
    labels = []
    ids = []
    cls = []

    print('Reading training images')
    for fld in classes:
        index = classes.index(fld)
        print('Loading {} files (Index: {})'.format(fld, index))
        path = os.path.join(train_path, fld, '*g')
        files = glob.glob(path)
        for fl in files:
            image = cv2.imread(fl)
            image = cv2.resize(image, (image_size, image_size),
    cv2.INTER_LINEAR)
            images.append(image)
            label = np.zeros(len(classes))
            label[index] = 1.0
            labels.append(label)
            flbase = os.path.basename(fl)
            ids.append(flbase)
            cls.append(fld)
    images = np.array(images)
    labels = np.array(labels)
    ids = np.array(ids)
    cls = np.array(cls)
    return images, labels, ids, cls
```

The `DataSet` class, which is used to generate the batches of the training set, is as follows:

```
class DataSet(object):
  def next_batch(self, batch_size):
    """Return the next `batch_size` examples from this data set."""
    start = self._index_in_epoch
    self._index_in_epoch += batch_size
    if self._index_in_epoch > self._num_examples:
      # Finished epoch
      self._epochs_completed += 1
      start = 0
      self._index_in_epoch = batch_size
      assert batch_size <= self._num_examples
    end = self._index_in_epoch
    return self._images[start:end], self._labels[start:end],
self._ids[start:end], self._cls[start:end]
```

Then, similarly, we prepare the test set from the test images that are mixed (dogs and cats):

```
test_images, test_ids = Preprocessor.read_test_set(test_path, img_size)
```

We have the `read_test_set()` function for ease, as follows:

```
def read_test_set(test_path, image_size):
  images, ids = load_test(test_path, image_size)
  return images, ids
```

Now, similar to the training set, we have a dedicated function called `load_test()` for loading the test set, which goes as follows:

```
def load_test(test_path, image_size):
  path = os.path.join(test_path, '*g')
  files = sorted(glob.glob(path))

  X_test = []
  X_test_id = []
  print("Reading test images")
  for fl in files:
      flbase = os.path.basename(fl)
      img = cv2.imread(fl)
      img = cv2.resize(img, (image_size, image_size), cv2.INTER_LINEAR)
      X_test.append(img)
      X_test_id.append(flbase)
  X_test = np.array(X_test, dtype=np.uint8)
  X_test = X_test.astype('float32')
  X_test = X_test / 255
  return X_test, X_test_id
```

Well done! We can now see some randomly selected images. For this, we have the helper function called `plot_images()`; it creates a figure with 3 x 3 sub-plots. So, all together, nine images will be plotted, along with their true label. It goes as follows:

```python
def plot_images(images, cls_true, cls_pred=None):
    if len(images) == 0:
        print("no images to show")
        return
    else:
        random_indices = random.sample(range(len(images)), min(len(images),
9))

        images, cls_true  = zip(*[(images[i], cls_true[i]) for i in
random_indices])
    fig, axes = plt.subplots(3, 3)
    fig.subplots_adjust(hspace=0.3, wspace=0.3)
    for i, ax in enumerate(axes.flat):
        # Plot image.
        ax.imshow(images[i].reshape(img_size, img_size, num_channels))
        if cls_pred is None:
            xlabel = "True: {0}".format(cls_true[i])
        else:
            xlabel = "True: {0}, Pred: {1}".format(cls_true[i],
cls_pred[i])
        ax.set_xlabel(xlabel)
        ax.set_xticks([])
        ax.set_yticks([])
    plt.show()
```

Let's get some random images and their labels from the train set:

```python
images, cls_true  = data.train.images, data.train.cls
```

Finally, we plot the images and labels using our helper-function in the preceding code:

```python
plot_images(images=images, cls_true=cls_true)
```

The preceding line of code generates the true labels of the images that are randomly selected:

Figure 6: The true labels of the images that are randomly selected

Finally, we can print the dataset statistics:

```
print("Size of:")
print("   - Training-set:tt{}".format(len(data.train.labels)))
print("   - Test-set:tt{}".format(len(test_images)))
print("   - Validation-set:t{}".format(len(data.valid.labels)))

>>>
Reading training images
 Loading dogs files (Index: 0)
 Loading cats files (Index: 1)
 Reading test images
 Size of:
 - Training-set: 21000
 - Test-set: 12500
 - Validation-set: 4000
```

# Step 3- Defining CNN hyperparameters

Now that we have the training and test set, it's time to define the hyperparameters for the CNN model before we start constructing. In the first and the second convolutional layers, we define the width and height of each filter, that is, 3, where the number of filters is 32:

```
filter_size1 = 3
num_filters1 = 32
filter_size2 = 3
num_filters2 = 32
```

The third convolutional layer has equal dimensions but twice the filters; that is, 64 filters:

```
filter_size3 = 3
num_filters3 = 64
```

The last two layers are fully connected layers, specifying the number of neurons:

```
fc_size = 128
```

Now let's make the training slower for more intensive training by setting a lower value of the learning rate, as follows:

```
learning_rate=1e-4
```

# Step 4 – Constructing the CNN layers

Once we have defined the CNN hyperparameters, the next task is to implement the CNN network. As you can guess, for our task, we will construct a CNN network having three convolutional layers, a flattened layer and two fully connected layers (refer to LayersConstructor.py). Moreover, we need to define the weight and the bias as well. Furthermore, we will have implicit max-pooling layers too. At first, let's define the weight. In the following, we have the new_weights() method that asks for the image shape and returns the truncated normal shapes:

```
def new_weights(shape):
    return tf.Variable(tf.truncated_normal(shape, stddev=0.05))
```

Then we define the biases using the new_biases() method:

```
def new_biases(length):
    return tf.Variable(tf.constant(0.05, shape=[length]))
```

Now let's define a method, `new_conv_layer()`, for constructing a convolutional layer. The method takes the input batch, number of input channels, filter size, and number of filters and it also uses the max pooling (if true, we use a 2 x 2 max pooling) to construct a new convolutional layer. The workflow of the method is as follows:

1. Define the shape of the filter weights for the convolution, which is determined by the TensorFlow API.

2. Create the new weights (that is, filters) with the given shape and new biases, one for each filter.

3. Create the TensorFlow operation for the convolution where the strides are set to 1 in all dimensions. The first and last stride must always be 1, because the first is for the image-number and the last is for the input channel. For example, strides= (1, 2, 2, 1) would mean that the filter is moved two pixels across the $x$ axis and $y$ axis of the image.

4. Add the biases to the results of the convolution. Then a bias-value is added to each filter-channel.

5. It then uses the pooling to downsample the image resolution. This is 2 x 2 max pooling, which means that we consider 2 x 2 windows and select the largest value in each window. Then we move two pixels to the next window.

6. ReLU is then used to calculate the $max(x, 0)$ for each input pixel $x$. As stated earlier, a ReLU is normally executed before the pooling, but since `relu(max_pool(x)) == max_pool(relu(x))` we can save 75% of the relu-operations by max-pooling first.

7. Finally, it returns both the resulting layer and the filter-weights because we will plot the weights later.

Now we define a function to construct the convolutional layer to be used:

```
def new_conv_layer(input,   num_input_channels, filter_size, num_filters,
use_pooling=True):
    shape = [filter_size, filter_size, num_input_channels, num_filters]
    weights = new_weights(shape=shape)
    biases = new_biases(length=num_filters)
    layer = tf.nn.conv2d(input=input,
                         filter=weights,
                         strides=[1, 1, 1, 1],
                         padding='SAME')
    layer += biases
    if use_pooling:
        layer = tf.nn.max_pool(value=layer,
                               ksize=[1, 2, 2, 1],
                               strides=[1, 2, 2, 1],
```

```
                              padding='SAME')
    layer = tf.nn.relu(layer)
    return layer, weights
```

The next task is to define the flattened layer:

1. Get the shape of the input layer.
2. The number of features is `img_height` * `img_width` * `num_channels`. The `get_shape()` function TensorFlow is used to calculate this.
3. It will then reshape the layer to (`num_images` and `num_features`). We just set the size of the second dimension to `num_features` and the size of the first dimension to -1, which means the size in that dimension is calculated so the total size of the tensor is unchanged from the reshaping.
4. Finally, it returns both the flattened layer and the number of features.

The following code does exactly the same as described before `def flatten_layer(layer):`

```
    layer_shape = layer.get_shape()
    num_features = layer_shape[1:4].num_elements()
    layer_flat = tf.reshape(layer, [-1, num_features])
    return layer_flat, num_features
```

Finally, we need to construct the fully connected layers. The following function, `new_fc_layer()`, takes the input batches, number of batches, and number of outputs (that is, predicted classes) and it uses the ReLU. It then creates the weights and biases based on the methods we define earlier in this step. Finally, it calculates the layer as the matrix multiplication of the input and weights, and then adds the bias values:

```
def new_fc_layer(input, num_inputs, num_outputs, use_relu=True):
    weights = new_weights(shape=[num_inputs, num_outputs])
    biases = new_biases(length=num_outputs)
    layer = tf.matmul(input, weights) + biases
    if use_relu:
        layer = tf.nn.relu(layer)
    return layer
```

# Step 5 – Preparing the TensorFlow graph

We now create the placeholders for the TensorFlow graph:

```
x = tf.placeholder(tf.float32, shape=[None, img_size_flat], name='x')
x_image = tf.reshape(x, [-1, img_size, img_size, num_channels])
y_true = tf.placeholder(tf.float32, shape=[None, num_classes],
name='y_true')
y_true_cls = tf.argmax(y_true, axis=1)
```

# Step 6 – Creating a CNN model

Now we have the input; that is, x_image is ready to feed to the convolutional layer. We formally create a convolutional layer, followed by the max pooling:

```
layer_conv1, weights_conv1 =
    LayersConstructor.new_conv_layer(input=x_image,
                    num_input_channels=num_channels,
                    filter_size=filter_size1,
                    num_filters=num_filters1,
                    use_pooling=True)
```

We must have the second convolutional layer, where the input is the first convolutional layer, layer_conv1, followed by the max pooling:

```
layer_conv2, weights_conv2 =
    LayersConstructor.new_conv_layer(input=layer_conv1,
                    num_input_channels=num_filters1,
                    filter_size=filter_size2,
                    num_filters=num_filters2,
                    use_pooling=True)
```

We now have the third convolutional layer where the input is the output of the second convolutional layer, that is, layer_conv2 followed by the max pooling:

```
layer_conv3, weights_conv3 =
    LayersConstructor.new_conv_layer(input=layer_conv2,
                    num_input_channels=num_filters2,
                    filter_size=filter_size3,
                    num_filters=num_filters3,
                    use_pooling=True)
```

Once the third convolutional layer is instantiated, we then instantiate the flattened layer as follows:

```
layer_flat, num_features = LayersConstructor.flatten_layer(layer_conv3)
```

Once we have flattened the images, they are ready to be fed to the first fully connected layer. We use the ReLU:

```
layer_fc1 = LayersConstructor.new_fc_layer(input=layer_flat,
                    num_inputs=num_features,
                    num_outputs=fc_size,
                    use_relu=True)
```

Finally, we have to have the second and the final fully connected layer where the input is the output of the first fully connected layer:

```
layer_fc2 = LayersConstructor.new_fc_layer(input=layer_fc1,
                    num_inputs=fc_size,
                    num_outputs=num_classes,
                    use_relu=False)
```

# Step 7 – Running the TensorFlow graph to train the CNN model

The following steps are used to perform the training. The codes are self-explanatory, like the ones that we have already used in our previous examples. We use softmax to predict the classes by comparing them with true classes:

```
y_pred = tf.nn.softmax(layer_fc2)
y_pred_cls = tf.argmax(y_pred, axis=1)
cross_entropy =
tf.nn.softmax_cross_entropy_with_logits_v2(logits=layer_fc2,
labels=y_true)
```

We define the `cost` function and then the optimizer (Adam optimizer in this case). Then we compute the accuracy:

```
cost_op= tf.reduce_mean(cross_entropy)
optimizer =
tf.train.AdamOptimizer(learning_rate=learning_rate).minimize(cost_op)
correct_prediction = tf.equal(y_pred_cls, y_true_cls)
accuracy = tf.reduce_mean(tf.cast(correct_prediction, tf.float32))
```

Then we initialize all the ops using the `global_variables_initializer()` function from TensorFlow:

```
init_op = tf.global_variables_initializer()
```

Then we create and run the TensorFlow session to carry the training across the tensors:

```
session = tf.Session()
session.run(init_op)
```

We then feed out training data so that the batch size to 32 (see *Step 2*):

```
train_batch_size = batch_size
```

We maintain two lists to track the training and validation accuracy:

```
acc_list = []
val_acc_list = []
```

We then count the total number of iterations performed so far and create an empty list to keep track of all the iterations:

```
total_iterations = 0
iter_list = []
```

We formally start the training by invoking the `optimize()` function, which takes a number of iterations. It needs two:

- The `x_batch` of training examples that holds a batch of images and
- `y_true_batch`, the true labels for those images

It then converts the shape of each image from (num examples, rows, columns, depth) to (num examples, flattened image shape). After that, we put the batch into a `dict` for placeholder variables in the TensorFlow graph. Later on, we run the optimizer on the batch of training data.

Then, TensorFlow assigns the variables in `feed_dict_train` to the placeholder variables. Optimizer is then executed to print the status at end of each epoch. Finally, it updates the total number of iterations that we performed:

```
def optimize(num_iterations):
    global total_iterations
    best_val_loss = float("inf")
    patience = 0
    for i in range(total_iterations, total_iterations + num_iterations):
        x_batch, y_true_batch, _, cls_batch =
```

```
data.train.next_batch(train_batch_size)
        x_valid_batch, y_valid_batch, _, valid_cls_batch =
data.valid.next_batch(train_batch_size)
        x_batch = x_batch.reshape(train_batch_size, img_size_flat)
        x_valid_batch = x_valid_batch.reshape(train_batch_size,
img_size_flat)
        feed_dict_train = {x: x_batch, y_true: y_true_batch}
        feed_dict_validate = {x: x_valid_batch, y_true: y_valid_batch}
        session.run(optimizer, feed_dict=feed_dict_train)

        if i % int(data.train.num_examples/batch_size) == 0:
            val_loss = session.run(cost, feed_dict=feed_dict_validate)
            epoch = int(i / int(data.train.num_examples/batch_size))
            acc, val_acc = print_progress(epoch, feed_dict_train,
feed_dict_validate, val_loss)
            acc_list.append(acc)
            val_acc_list.append(val_acc)
            iter_list.append(epoch+1)
            if early_stopping:
                if val_loss < best_val_loss:
                    best_val_loss = val_loss
                    patience = 0
                else:
                    patience += 1
                if patience == early_stopping:
                    break
    total_iterations += num_iterations
```

We will show how our training went along in the next section.

## Step 8 – Model evaluation

We have managed to finish the training. It is time to evaluate the model. Before, we start evaluating the model, let's implement some auxiliary functions for plotting the example errors and printing the validation accuracy. The plot_example_errors() takes two parameters. The first is cls_pred, which is an array of the predicted class-number for all images in the test set.

The second parameter, `correct`, is a `boolean` array to predict whether the predicted class is equal to `true` class for each image in the test set. At first, it gets the images from the test set that have been incorrectly classified. Then it gets the predicted and the true classes for those images, and finally it plots the first nine images with their classes (that is, predicted versus true labels):

```
def plot_example_errors(cls_pred, correct):
    incorrect = (correct == False)
    images = data.valid.images[incorrect]
    cls_pred = cls_pred[incorrect]
    cls_true = data.valid.cls[incorrect]
    plot_images(images=images[0:9], cls_true=cls_true[0:9],
cls_pred=cls_pred[0:9])
```

The second auxiliary function is called `print_validation_accuracy()`; it prints the validation accuracy. It allocates an array for the predicted classes, which will be calculated in batches and filled into this array, and then it calculates the predicted classes for the batches:

```
def print_validation_accuracy(show_example_errors=False,
show_confusion_matrix=False):
    num_test = len(data.valid.images)
    cls_pred = np.zeros(shape=num_test, dtype=np.int)
    i = 0
    while i < num_test:
        # The ending index for the next batch is denoted j.
        j = min(i + batch_size, num_test)
        images = data.valid.images[i:j, :].reshape(batch_size,
img_size_flat)
        labels = data.valid.labels[i:j, :]
        feed_dict = {x: images, y_true: labels}
        cls_pred[i:j] = session.run(y_pred_cls, feed_dict=feed_dict)
        i = j

    cls_true = np.array(data.valid.cls)
    cls_pred = np.array([classes[x] for x in cls_pred])
    correct = (cls_true == cls_pred)
    correct_sum = correct.sum()
    acc = float(correct_sum) / num_test

    msg = "Accuracy on Test-Set: {0:.1%} ({1} / {2})"
    print(msg.format(acc, correct_sum, num_test))

    if show_example_errors:
        print("Example errors:")
        plot_example_errors(cls_pred=cls_pred, correct=correct)
```

Now that we have our auxiliary functions, we can start the optimization. At the first place, let's iterate the fine-tuning 10,000 times and see the performance:

```
optimize(num_iterations=1000)
```

After 10,000 iterations, we observe the following result:

```
Accuracy on Test-Set: 78.8% (3150 / 4000)
Precision: 0.793378626929
Recall: 0.7875
F1-score: 0.786639298213
```

This means the accuracy on the test set is about 79%. Also, let's see how well our classifier performs on a sample image:

Figure 7: Random prediction on the test set (after 10,000 iterations)

After that, we further iterate the optimization up to 100,000 times and observe better accuracy:

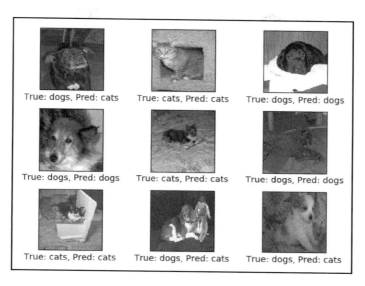

Figure 8: Random prediction on the test set (after 100,000 iterations)

```
>>>
Accuracy on Test-Set: 81.1% (3244 / 4000)
Precision: 0.811057239265
Recall: 0.811
F1-score: 0.81098298755
```

So it did not improve that much but was a 2% increase on the overall accuracy. Now is the time to evaluate our model for a single image. For simplicity, we will take two random images of a dog and a cat and see the prediction power of our model:

Figure 9: Example image for the cat and dog to be classified

At first, we load these two images and prepare the test set accordingly, as we have seen in an earlier step in this example:

```
test_cat = cv2.imread('Test_image/cat.jpg')
test_cat = cv2.resize(test_cat, (img_size, img_size), cv2.INTER_LINEAR) /
255
preview_cat = plt.imshow(test_cat.reshape(img_size, img_size,
num_channels))

test_dog = cv2.imread('Test_image/dog.jpg')
test_dog = cv2.resize(test_dog, (img_size, img_size), cv2.INTER_LINEAR) /
255
preview_dog = plt.imshow(test_dog.reshape(img_size, img_size,
num_channels))
```

Then we have the following function for making the prediction:

```
def sample_prediction(test_im):
    feed_dict_test = {
        x: test_im.reshape(1, img_size_flat),
        y_true: np.array([[1, 0]])
    }
    test_pred = session.run(y_pred_cls, feed_dict=feed_dict_test)
    return classes[test_pred[0]]
print("Predicted class for test_cat:
{}".format(sample_prediction(test_cat)))
print("Predicted class for test_dog:
{}".format(sample_prediction(test_dog)))

>>>
Predicted class for test_cat: cats
Predicted class for test_dog: dogs
```

Finally, when we're done, we close the TensorFlow session by invoking the `close()` method:

```
session.close()
```

# Model performance optimization

Since CNNs are different from the layering architecture's perspective, they have different requirements as well as tuning criteria. How do you know what combination of hyperparameters is the best for your task? Of course, you can use a grid search with cross-validation to find the right hyperparameters for linear machine learning models.

However, for CNNs, there are many hyperparameters to tune, and since training a neural network on a large dataset takes a lot of time, you will only be able to explore a tiny part of the hyperparameter space in a reasonable amount of time. Here are some insights that can be followed.

# Number of hidden layers

For many problems, you can just begin with a single hidden layer and you will get reasonable results. It has actually been shown that an MLP with just one hidden layer can model even the most complex functions provided it has enough neurons. For a long time, these facts convinced researchers that there was no need to investigate any deeper neural networks. However, they overlooked the fact that deep networks have a much higher parameter efficiency than shallow ones; they can model complex functions using exponentially fewer neurons than shallow nets, making them much faster to train.

It is to be noted that this might not be always the case. However, in summary, for many problems, you can start with just one or two hidden layers. It will work just fine using two hidden layers with the same total amount of neurons, in roughly the same amount of training time. For a more complex problem, you can gradually ramp up the number of hidden layers, until you start overfitting the training set. Very complex tasks, such as large image classification or speech recognition, typically require networks with dozens of layers and a huge amount of training data.

# Number of neurons per hidden layer

Obviously, the number of neurons in the input and output layers is determined by the type of input and output your task requires. For example, if your dataset has the shape of 28 x 28 it should expect to have input neurons with size 784 and the output neurons should be equal to the number of classes to be predicted. As for the hidden layers, a common practice is to size them to form a funnel, with fewer and fewer neurons at each layer, the rationale being that many low-level features can coalesce into far fewer high-level features. However, this practice is not as common now, and you may simply use the same size for all hidden layers.

If there are four convolutional layers with 256 neurons, that's just one hyperparameter to tune instead of one per layer. Just like the number of layers, you can try increasing the number of neurons gradually until the network starts overfitting. Another important question is: when would you want to add a max pooling layer rather than a convolutional layer with the same stride? The thing is that a max-pooling layer has no parameters at all, whereas a convolutional layer has quite a few.

Sometimes, adding a local response normalization layer that makes the neurons that most strongly activate inhibit neurons at the same location but in neighboring feature maps, encourages different feature maps to specialize and pushes them apart, forcing them to explore a wider range of features. It is typically used in the lower layers to have a larger pool of low-level features that the upper layers can build upon.

# Batch normalization

**Batch normalization** (**BN**) is a method to reduce internal covariate shift while training regular DNNs. This can apply to CNNs too. Due to the normalization, BN further prevents smaller changes to the parameters to amplify and thereby allows higher learning rates, making the network even faster:

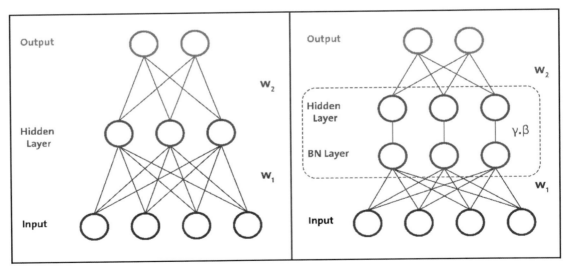

The idea is placing an additional step between the layers, in which the output of the layer before is normalized. To be more specific, in the case of non-linear operations (for example, ReLU), BN transformation has to be applied to the non-linear operation. Typically, the overall process has the following workflow:

- Transforming the network into a BN network (see *Figure 1*)
- Then training the new network
- Transforming the batch statistic into a population statistic

This way, BN can fully partake in the process of backpropagation. As shown in *Figure 1*, BN is performed before the other processes of the network in this layer are applied. However, any kind of gradient descent (for example, **stochastic gradient descent (SGD)** and its variants) can be applied to train the BN network.

 Interested readers can refer to the original paper to get to more information: Ioffe, Sergey, and Christian Szegedy. *Batch normalization: Accelerating deep network training by reducing internal covariate shift.* arXiv preprint arXiv:1502.03167 (2015).

Now a valid question would be: where to place the BN layer? Well, to know the answer, a quick evaluation of BatchNorm layer performance on ImageNet-2012 (`https://github.com/ducha-aiki/caffenet-benchmark/blob/master/batchnorm.md`) shows the following benchmark:

| Name | Accuracy | LogLoss | Comments |
| --- | --- | --- | --- |
| Before | 0.474 | 2.35 | As in paper |
| Before + scale&bias layer | 0.478 | 2.33 | As in paper |
| After | 0.499 | 2.21 | |
| After + scale&bias layer | 0.493 | 2.24 | |

From the preceding table, it can be seen that placing BN after non-linearity would be the right way. The second question would be: what activation function should be used in a BN layer? Well, from the same benchmark, we can see the following result:

| Name | Accuracy | LogLoss | Comments |
|---|---|---|---|
| ReLU | 0.499 | 2.21 | |
| RReLU | 0.500 | 2.20 | |
| PReLU | 0.503 | 2.19 | |
| ELU | 0.498 | 2.23 | |
| Maxout | 0.487 | 2.28 | |
| Sigmoid | 0.475 | 2.35 | |
| TanH | 0.448 | 2.50 | |
| No | 0.384 | 2.96 | |

From the preceding table, we can assume that using ReLU or its variants would be a better idea. Now, another question would be how to use these using deep learning libraries. Well, in TensorFlow, it is:

```
training = tf.placeholder(tf.bool)
x = tf.layers.dense(input_x, units=100)
x = tf.layers.batch_normalization(x, training=training)
x = tf.nn.relu(x)
```

A general warning: set this to `True` for training and `False` for testing. However, the preceding addition introduces extra ops to be performed on the graph, which is updating its mean and variance variables in such a way that they will not be dependencies of your training op. To do it, we can just run the ops separately, as follows:

```
extra_update_ops = tf.get_collection(tf.GraphKeys.UPDATE_OPS)
sess.run([train_op, extra_update_ops], ...)
```

# Advanced regularization and avoiding overfitting

As mentioned in the previous chapter, one of the main disadvantages observed during the training of large neural networks is overfitting, that is, generating very good approximations for the training data but emitting noise for the zones between single points. There are a couple of ways to reduce or even prevent this issue, such as dropout, early stop, and limiting the number of parameters.

In the case of overfitting, the model is specifically adjusted to the training dataset, so it will not be used for generalization. Therefore, although it performs well on the training set, its performance on the test dataset and subsequent tests is poor because it lacks the generalization property:

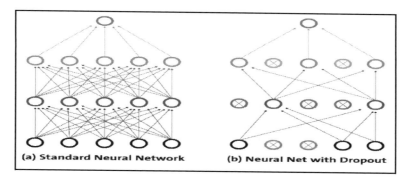

Figure 10: Dropout versus without dropout

The main advantage of this method is that it avoids holding all the neurons in a layer to optimize their weights synchronously. This adaptation made in random groups prevents all the neurons from converging to the same goals, thus de-correlating the adapted weights. A second property found in the dropout application is that the activation of the hidden units becomes sparse, which is also a desirable characteristic.

In the preceding figure, we have a representation of an original fully connected multilayer neural network and the associated network with the dropout linked. As a result, approximately half of the input was zeroed (this example was chosen to show that probabilities will not always give the expected four zeroes). One factor that could have surprised you is the scale factor applied to the non-dropped elements.

This technique is used to maintain the same network, and restore it to the original architecture when training, using `dropout_keep_prob` as 1. A major drawback of using dropout is that it does not have the same benefits for convolutional layers, where the neurons are not fully connected. To address this issue, there are a few techniques can be applied, such as DropConnect and stochastic pooling:

- DropConnect is similar to dropout as it introduces dynamic sparsity within the model, but it differs in that the sparsity is on the weights, rather than the output vectors of a layer. The thing is that a fully connected layer with DropConnect becomes a sparsely connected layer in which the connections are chosen at random during the training stage.
- In stochastic pooling, the conventional deterministic pooling operations are replaced with a stochastic procedure, where the activation within each pooling region is picked randomly according to a multinomial distribution, given by the activities within the pooling region. The approach is hyperparameter free and can be combined with other regularization approaches, such as dropout and data augmentation.

**Stochastic pooling versus standard max pooling:** Stochastic pooling is equivalent to standard max pooling but with many copies of an input image, each having small local deformations.

Secondly, one of the simplest methods to prevent overfitting of a network is to simply stop the training before overfitting gets a chance to occur. This comes with the disadvantage that the learning process is halted. Thirdly, limiting the number of parameters is sometimes helpful and helps avoid overfitting. When it comes to CNN training, the filter size also affects the number of parameters. Thus, limiting this type of parameter restricts the predictive power of the network directly, reducing the complexity of the function that it can perform on the data, and that limits the amount of overfitting.

# Applying dropout operations with TensorFlow

If we apply the dropout operation to a sample vector, it will work on transmitting the dropout to all the architecture-dependent units. In order to apply the dropout operation, TensorFlow implements the `tf.nn.dropout` method, which works as follows:

```
tf.nn.dropout (x, keep_prob, noise_shape, seed, name)
```

Where x is the original tensor. The `keep_prob` means the probability of keeping a neuron and the factor by which the remaining nodes are multiplied. The `noise_shape` signifies a four-element list that determines whether a dimension will apply zeroing independently or not. Let's have a look at this code segment:

```
import tensorflow as tf X = [1.5, 0.5, 0.75, 1.0, 0.75, 0.6, 0.4, 0.9]
drop_out = tf.nn.dropout(X, 0.5)
sess = tf.Session() with sess.as_default():
    print(drop_out.eval())
sess.close()

[ 3. 0. 1.5 0. 0. 1.20000005 0. 1.79999995]
```

In the preceding example, you can see the results of applying dropout to the *x* variable, with a 0.5 probability of zero; in the cases in which it didn't occur, the values were doubled (multiplied by 1/1.5, the dropout probability).

# Which optimizer to use?

When using a CNN, since one of the objective functions is to minimize the evaluated cost, we must define an optimizer. Using the most common optimizer , such as SGD, the learning rates must scale with *1/T* to get convergence, where *T* is the number of iterations. Adam or RMSProp try to overcome this limitation automatically by adjusting the step size so that the step is on the same scale as the gradients. In addition, in the previous example, we have used Adam optimizer, which performs well in most cases.

Nevertheless, if you are training a neural network but computing the gradients is mandatory, using the `RMSPropOptimizer` function (which implements the `RMSProp` algorithm) is a better idea since it would be the faster way of learning in a mini-batch setting. Researchers also recommend using the momentum optimizer, while training a deep CNN or DNN. Technically, `RMSPropOptimizer` is an advanced form of gradient descent that divides the learning rate by an exponentially decaying average of squared gradients. The suggested setting value of the decay parameter is 0.9, while a good default value for the learning rate is 0.001. For example, in TensorFlow, `tf.train.RMSPropOptimizer()` helps us to use this with ease:

```
optimizer = tf.train.RMSPropOptimizer(0.001, 0.9).minimize(cost_op)
```

# Memory tuning

In this section, we try to provide some insights. We start with an issue and its solution; convolutional layers require a huge amount of RAM, especially during training, because the reverse pass of backpropagation requires all the intermediate values computed during the forward pass. During inference (that is, when making a prediction for a new instance), the RAM occupied by one layer can be released as soon as the next layer has been computed, so you only need as much RAM as required by two consecutive layers.

Nevertheless, during training, everything computed during the forward pass needs to be preserved for the reverse pass, so the amount of RAM needed is (at least) the total amount of RAM required by all layers. If your GPU runs out of memory while training a CNN, here are five things you can try to solve the problem (other than purchasing a GPU with more RAM):

- Reduce the mini-batch size
- Reduce dimensionality using a larger stride in one or more layers
- Remove one or more layers
- Use 16-bit floats instead of 32-bit
- Distribute the CNN across multiple devices (see more at `https://www.tensorflow.org/deploy/distributed`)

# Appropriate layer placement

Another important question would be: when do you want to add a max pooling layer rather than a convolutional layer with the same stride? The thing is that a max-pooling layer has no parameters at all, whereas a convolutional layer has quite a few.

Even adding a local response normalization layer sometimes makes the neurons that most strongly activate inhibit neurons at the same location but in neighboring feature maps, which encourages different feature maps to specialize and pushes them apart, forcing them to explore a wider range of features. It is typically used in the lower layers to have a larger pool of low-level features that the upper layers can build upon.

# Building the second CNN by putting everything together

Now we know how to optimize the layering structure in a CNN by adding dropout, BN, and biases initializers, such as Xavier. Let's try to apply these to a less complex CNN. Throughout this example, we will see how to solve a real-life classification problem. To be more specific, our CNN model will be able to classify the traffic sign from a bunch of images.

## Dataset description and preprocessing

For this we will be using the Belgian traffic dataset (BelgiumTS for Classification (cropped images)). This dataset can be download from `http://btsd.ethz.ch/shareddata/`. Here are a quick glimpse about the traffic signs convention in Belgium:

- Belgian traffic signs are usually in Dutch and French. This is good to know, but for the dataset that you'll be working with, it's not too important!
- There are six categories of traffic signs in Belgium: warning signs, priority signs, prohibitory signs, mandatory signs, signs related to parking and standing still on the road and, lastly, designatory signs.

Once we download the aforementioned dataset, we will see the following directory structure (training left, test right):

| Desktop › BelgiumTSC_Training › Training | | Desktop › BelgiumTSC_Testing › Testing | |
|---|---|---|---|
| 00000 | 00037 | 00000 | 00037 |
| 00001 | 00038 | 00001 | 00038 |
| 00002 | 00039 | 00002 | 00039 |
| 00003 | 00040 | 00003 | 00040 |
| 00004 | 00041 | 00004 | 00041 |
| 00005 | 00042 | 00005 | 00042 |
| 00006 | 00043 | 00006 | 00043 |
| 00007 | 00044 | 00007 | 00044 |

The images are in .ppm format; otherwise we could've used TensorFlow built-in image loader (example, tf.image.decode_png). However, we can use the skimage Python package.

In Python 3, execute $ sudo pip3 install scikit-image for skimage to install and use this package. So let's get started by showing the directory path as follows:

```
Train_IMAGE_DIR = "<path>/BelgiumTSC_Training/"
Test_IMAGE_DIR = ""<path>/BelgiumTSC_Testing/"
```

Then let's write a function using the skimage library to read the images and returns two lists:

- images: A list of Numpy arrays, each representing an image
- labels: A list of numbers that represent the images labels

```
def load_data(data_dir):
    # All subdirectories, where each folder represents a unique label
    directories = [d for d in os.listdir(data_dir)if
os.path.isdir(os.path.join(data_dir, d))]

    # Iterate label directories and collect data in two lists, labels and
images.
    labels = []
    images = []
    for d in directories:label_dir = os.path.join(data_dir, d)
    file_names = [os.path.join(label_dir, f)
                for f in os.listdir(label_dir) if f.endswith(".ppm")]

    # For each label, load it's images and add them to the images list.
    # And add the label number (i.e. directory name) to the labels list.
    for f in file_names:images.append(skimage.data.imread(f))
    labels.append(int(d))
    return images, labels
```

The preceding code block is straightforward and contains inline comments. How about showing related statistics about images? However, before that, let's invoke the preceding function:

```
# Load training and testing datasets.
train_data_dir = os.path.join(Train_IMAGE_DIR, "Training")
test_data_dir = os.path.join(Test_IMAGE_DIR, "Testing")

images, labels = load_data(train_data_dir)
```

Then let's see some statistics:

```
print("Unique classes: {0} \nTotal Images: {1}".format(len(set(labels)),
len(images)))

>>>
Unique classes: 62
Total Images: 4575
```

So we have 62 classes to be predicted (that is, a multiclass image classification problem) and we have many images too that should be sufficient to satisfy a smaller CNN. Now let's see the class distribution visually:

```
# Make a histogram with 62 bins of the `labels` data and show the plot:
plt.hist(labels, 62)
plt.xlabel('Class')
plt.ylabel('Number of training examples')
plt.show()
```

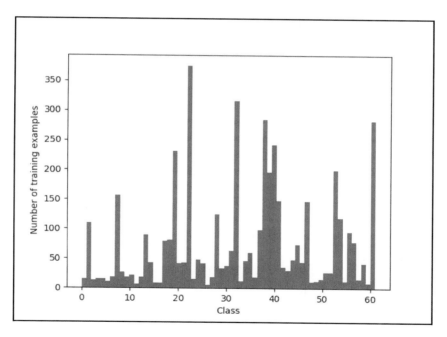

Therefore, from the preceding figure, we can see that classes are very imbalanced. However, to make it simpler, we won't take care of this but next, it would be great to visually inspect some files, say displaying the first image of each label:

```
def display_images_and_labels(images, labels):
    unique_labels = set(labels)
    plt.figure(figsize=(15, 15))
    i = 1
    for label in unique_labels:
        # Pick the first image for each label.
        image = images[labels.index(label)]
        plt.subplot(8, 8, i) # A grid of 8 rows x 8 column
        splt.axis('off')
        plt.title("Label {0} ({1})".format(label, labels.count(label)))
        i += 1
        _= plt.imshow(image)
    plt.show()
display_images_and_labels(images, labels)
```

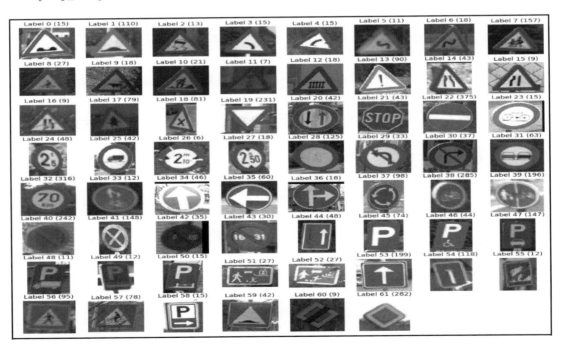

Now you can see from the preceding figure that the images come in different sizes and shapes. Moreover, we can see it using Python code, as follows:

```
for img in images[:5]:
    print("shape: {0}, min: {1}, max: {2}".format(img.shape, img.min(),
img.max()))

>>>
shape: (87, 84, 3), min: 12, max: 255
shape: (289, 169, 3), min: 0, max: 255
shape: (205, 76, 3), min: 0, max: 255
shape: (72, 71, 3), min: 14, max: 185
shape: (231, 228, 3), min: 0, max: 255
```

Therefore, we need to apply some pre-processing such as resizing, reshaping, and so on to each image. Let's say each image will have size of 32 x 32:

```
images32 = [skimage.transform.resize(img, (32, 32), mode='constant')

for img in images]for img in images32[:5]:
    print("shape: {0}, min: {1}, max: {2}".format(img.shape, img.min(),
img.max()))

>>>
shape: (32, 32, 3), min: 0.06642539828431372, max: 0.9704350490196079
shape: (32, 32, 3), min: 0.0, max: 1.0
shape: (32, 32, 3), min: 0.03172870710784261, max: 1.0
shape: (32, 32, 3), min: 0.059474571078431314, max: 0.7036305147058846
shape: (32, 32, 3), min: 0.01506204044117481, max: 1.0
```

Now, all of our images have same size. The next task would be to convert labels and image features as a numpy array:

```
labels_array = np.array(labels)
images_array = np.array(images32)
print("labels: ", labels_array.shape, "nimages: ", images_array.shape)

>>>
labels: (4575,)
images: (4575, 32, 32, 3)
```

Fantastic! The next task would be creating our second CNN, but this time we will be using TensorFlow contrib package, which is a high-level API that supports layering ops.

# Creating the CNN model

We are going to construct a complex network. However, it has a straightforward architecture. At the beginning, we use Xavier as the network initializer. Once we initialize the network bias using the Xavier initializer. The input layer is followed by a convolutional layer (convolutional layer 1), which is again followed by a BN layer (that is, BN layer 1). Then there is a pooling layer with strides of two and a kernel size of two. Then another BN layer follows the second convolutional layer. Next, there is the second pooling layer with strides of two and kernel size of two. Well, then the max polling layer is followed by a flattening layer that flattens the input from (None, height, width, channels) to (None, height * width * channels) == (None, 3072).

Once the flattening is completed, the input is fed into the first fully connected layer 1. Then third BN is applied as a normalizer function. Then we will have a dropout layer before we feed the lighter network into the fully connected layer 2 that generates logits of size (None, 62). Too much of a mouthful? Don't worry; we will see it step by step. Let's start the coding by creating the computational graph, creating both features, and labeling placeholders:

```
graph = tf.Graph()
with graph.as_default():
    # Placeholders for inputs and labels.
    images_X = tf.placeholder(tf.float32, [None, 32, 32, 3]) # each image's
32x32 size
    labels_X = tf.placeholder(tf.int32, [None])

    # Initializer: Xavier
    biasInit = tf.contrib.layers.xavier_initializer(uniform=True,
seed=None, dtype=tf.float32)

    # Convolution layer 1: number of neurons 128 and kernel size is 6x6.
    conv1 = tf.contrib.layers.conv2d(images_X, num_outputs=128,
kernel_size=[6, 6],
            biases_initializer=biasInit)

    # Batch normalization layer 1: can be applied as a normalizer
    # function for conv2d and fully_connected
    bn1 = tf.contrib.layers.batch_norm(conv1, center=True, scale=True,
is_training=True)

    # Max Pooling (down sampling) with strides of 2 and kernel size of 2
    pool1 = tf.contrib.layers.max_pool2d(bn1, 2, 2)

    # Convolution layer 2: number of neurons 256 and kernel size is 6x6.
    conv2 = tf.contrib.layers.conv2d(pool1, num_outputs=256,
kernel_size=[4, 4], stride=2,
```

```
                    biases_initializer=biasInit)

        # Batch normalization layer 2:
        bn2 = tf.contrib.layers.batch_norm(conv2, center=True, scale=True,
    is_training=True)

        # Max Pooling (down-sampling) with strides of 2 and kernel size of 2
        pool2 = tf.contrib.layers.max_pool2d(bn2, 2, 2)

        # Flatten the input from [None, height, width, channels] to
        # [None, height * width * channels] == [None, 3072]
        images_flat = tf.contrib.layers.flatten(pool2)

        # Fully connected layer 1
        fc1 = tf.contrib.layers.fully_connected(images_flat, 512, tf.nn.relu)

        # Batch normalization layer 3
        bn3 = tf.contrib.layers.batch_norm(fc1, center=True, scale=True,
    is_training=True)

        # apply dropout, if is_training is False, dropout is not applied
        fc1 = tf.layers.dropout(bn3, rate=0.25, training=True)

        # Fully connected layer 2 that generates logits of size [None, 62].
        # Here 62 means number of classes to be predicted.
        logits = tf.contrib.layers.fully_connected(fc1, 62, tf.nn.relu)
```

Up to this point, we have managed to generate the logits of size (None, 62). Then we need to convert the logits to label indexes (int) with the shape (None), which is a 1D vector of length == batch_size:predicted_labels = tf.argmax(logits, axis=1). Then we define cross-entropy as the loss function, which is a good choice for classification:

```
loss_op =
tf.reduce_mean(tf.nn.sparse_softmax_cross_entropy_with_logits(logits=logits
, labels=labels_X))
```

Now one of the most important parts is updating the ops and creating an optimizer (Adam in our case):

```
update_ops = tf.get_collection(tf.GraphKeys.UPDATE_OPS)
with tf.control_dependencies(update_ops):
    # Create an optimizer, which acts as the training op.train =
    tf.train.AdamOptimizer(learning_rate=0.10).minimize(loss_op)
```

Finally, we initialize all the ops:

```
init_op = tf.global_variables_initializer()
```

# Training and evaluating the network

We start by create a session to run the graph we created. Note that for faster training, we should use a GPU. However, if you do not have a GPU, just set `log_device_placement=False`:

```
session = tf.Session(graph=graph,
config=tf.ConfigProto(log_device_placement=True))
session.run(init_op)
for i in range(300):
    _, loss_value = session.run([train, loss_op], feed_dict={images_X:
images_array, labels_X:
    labels_array})
    if i % 10 == 0:
        print("Loss: ", loss_value)

>>>
Loss:  4.7910895
Loss:  4.3410876
Loss:  4.0275432
...
Loss:  0.523456
```

Once the training is completed, let us pick 10 random images and see the predictive power of our model:

```
random_indexes = random.sample(range(len(images32)), 10)
random_images = [images32[i]
for i in random_indexes]
    random_labels = [labels[i]
for i in random_indexes]
```

Then let's run the `predicted_labels` op:

```
predicted = session.run([predicted_labels], feed_dict={images_X:
random_images})[0]
print(random_labels)
print(predicted)

>>>
[38, 21, 19, 39, 22, 22, 45, 18, 22, 53]
[20  21  19  51  22  22  45  53  22  53]
```

So we can see that some images were correctly classified and some wrongly. However, visual inspection would be more helpful. So let's display the predictions and the ground truth:

```
fig = plt.figure(figsize=(5, 5))
for i in range(len(random_images)):
    truth = random_labels[i]
    prediction = predicted[i]
    plt.subplot(5, 2,1+i)
    plt.axis('off')color='green'
    if truth == prediction
    else
      'red'plt.text(40, 10, "Truth: {0}nPrediction: {1}".format(truth,
prediction), fontsize=12,
    color=color)
plt.imshow(random_images[i])
>>>
```

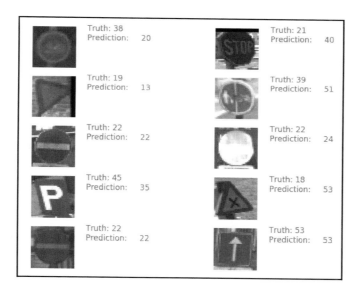

Finally, we can evaluate our model using the test set. To see the predictive power, we compute the accuracy:

```
# Load the test dataset.
test_X, test_y = load_data(test_data_dir)

# Transform the images, just as we did with the training set.
test_images32 = [skimage.transform.resize(img, (32, 32), mode='constant')
for img in test_X]
```

```
    display_images_and_labels(test_images32, test_y)

# Run predictions against the test
setpredicted = session.run([predicted_labels], feed_dict={images_X:
test_images32})[0]

# Calculate how many matches
match_count = sum([int(y == y_) for y, y_ in zip(test_y, predicted)])
accuracy = match_count / len(test_y)print("Accuracy:
{:.3f}".format(accuracy))

>>
Accuracy: 87.583
```

Not that bad in terms of accuracy. In addition to this, we can also compute other performance metrics such as precision, recall, f1 measure and also visualize the result in a confusion matrix to show the predicted versus actual labels count. Nevertheless, we can still improve the accuracy by tuning the network and hyperparameters. But I leave these up to the readers.

Finally, we are done, so let's close the TensorFlow session:

```
session.close()
```

# Summary

In this chapter, we discussed how to use CNNs, which are a type of feed-forward artificial neural network in which the connectivity pattern between neurons is inspired by the organization of an animal's visual cortex. We saw how to cascade a set of layers to construct a CNN and perform different operations in each layer. Then we saw how to train a CNN. Later on, we discussed how to optimize the CNN hyperparameters and optimization.

Finally, we built another CNN, where we utilized all the optimization techniques. Our CNN models did not achieve outstanding accuracy since we iterated both of the CNNs a few times and did not even apply any grid searching techniques; that means we did not hunt for the best combinations of the hyperparameters. Therefore, the takeaway would be to apply more robust feature engineering in the raw images, iterate the training for more epochs with the best hyperparameters, and observe the performance.

In the next chapter, we will see how to use some deeper and popular CNN architectures, such as ImageNet, AlexNet, VGG, GoogLeNet, and ResNet. We will see how to utilize these trained models for transfer learning.

# 4

# Popular CNN Model Architectures

In this chapter, will introduce the ImageNet image database and also cover the architectures of the following popular CNN models:

- LeNet
- AlexNet
- VGG
- GoogLeNet
- ResNet

## Introduction to ImageNet

ImageNet is a database of over 15 million hand-labeled, high-resolution images in roughly 22,000 categories. This database is organized just like the WordNet hierarchy, where each concept is also called a **synset** (that is, **synonym set**). Each synset is a node in the ImageNet hierarchy. Each node has more than 500 images.

The **ImageNet Large Scale Visual Recognition Challenge** (**ILSVRC**) was founded in 2010 to improve state-of-the-art technology for object detection and image classification on a large scale:

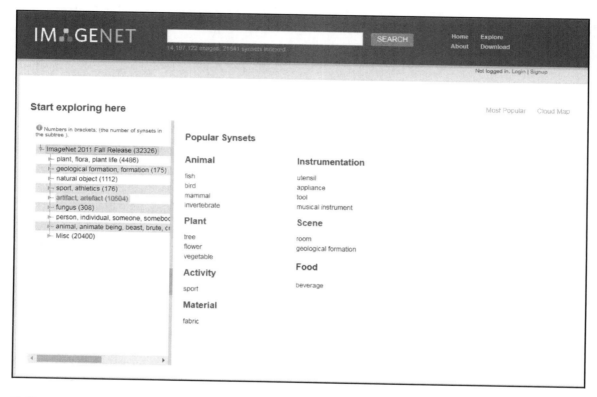

Following this overview of ImageNet, we will now take a look at various CNN model architectures.

# LeNet

In 2010, a challenge from ImageNet (known as **ILSVRC 2010**) came out with a CNN architecture, LeNet 5, built by Yann Lecun. This network takes a 32 x 32 image as input, which goes to the convolution layers (**C1**) and then to the subsampling layer (**S2**). Today, the subsampling layer is replaced by a pooling layer. Then, there is another sequence of convolution layers (**C3**) followed by a pooling (that is, subsampling) layer (**S4**). Finally, there are three fully connected layers, including the **OUTPUT** layer at the end. This network was used for zip code recognition in post offices. Since then, every year various CNN architectures were introduced with the help of this competition:

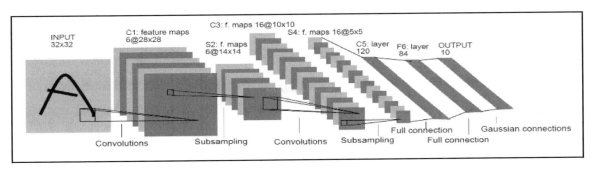

LeNet 5 – CNN architecture from Yann Lecun's article in 1998

Therefore, we can conclude the following points:

- The input to this network is a grayscale 32 x 32 image
- The architecture implemented is a CONV layer, followed by POOL and a fully connected layer
- CONV filters are 5 x 5, applied at a stride of 1

# AlexNet architecture

The first breakthrough in the architecture of CNN came in the year 2012. This award-winning CNN architecture is called **AlexNet**. It was developed at the University of Toronto by Alex Krizhevsky and his professor, Jeffry Hinton.

In the first run, a ReLU activation function and a dropout of 0.5 were used in this network to fight overfitting. As we can see in the following image, there is a normalization layer used in the architecture, but this is not used in practice anymore as it used heavy data augmentation. AlexNet is still used today even though there are more accurate networks available, because of its relative simple structure and small depth. It is widely used in computer vision:

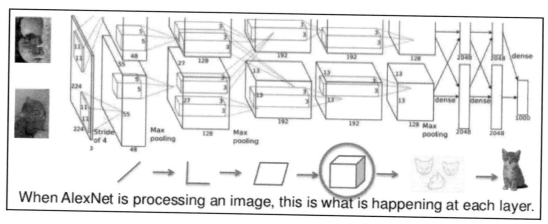

When AlexNet is processing an image, this is what is happening at each layer.

AlexNet is trained on the ImageNet database using two separate GPUs, possibly due to processing limitations with inter-GPU connections at the time, as shown in the following figure:

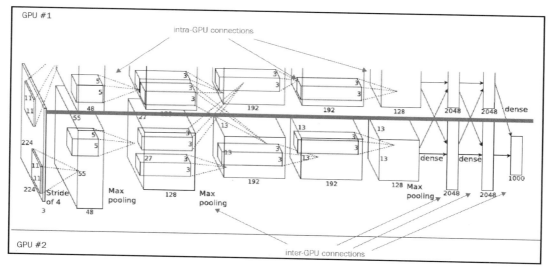

# Traffic sign classifiers using AlexNet

In this example, we will use transfer learning for feature extraction and a German traffic sign dataset to develop a classifier. Used here is an AlexNet implementation by Michael Guerzhoy and Davi Frossard, and AlexNet weights are from the Berkeley vision and Learning center. The complete code and dataset can be downloaded from here.

AlexNet expects a 227 x 227 x 3 pixel image, whereas the traffic sign images are 32 x 32 x 3 pixels. In order to feed the traffic sign images into AlexNet, we'll need to resize the images to the dimensions that AlexNet expects, that is, 227 x 227 x 3:

```
original_image = tf.placeholder(tf.float32, (None, 32, 32, 3))
resized_image = tf.image.resize_images(original_imag, (227, 227))
```

We can do so with the help of the `tf.image.resize_images` method by TensorFlow. Another issue here is that AlexNet was trained on the ImageNet dataset, which has 1,000 classes of images. So, we will replace this layer with a 43-neuron classification layer. To do this, figure out the size of the output from the last fully connected layer; since this is a fully connected layer and so is a 2D shape, the last element will be the size of the output. `fc7.get_shape().as_list()[-1]` does the trick; combine this with the number of classes for the traffic sign dataset to get the shape of the final fully connected layer: `shape = (fc7.get_shape().as_list()[-1], 43)`. The rest of the code is just the standard way to define a fully connected layer in TensorFlow. Finally, calculate the probabilities with `softmax`:

```
#Refer AlexNet implementation code, returns last fully connected layer
fc7 = AlexNet(resized, feature_extract=True)
shape = (fc7.get_shape().as_list()[-1], 43)
fc8_weight = tf.Variable(tf.truncated_normal(shape, stddev=1e-2))
fc8_b = tf.Variable(tf.zeros(43))
logits = tf.nn.xw_plus_b(fc7, fc8_weight, fc8_b)
probs = tf.nn.softmax(logits)
```

# VGGNet architecture

The runner-up in the 2014 ImageNet challenge was VGGNet from the visual geometric group at Oxford University. This convolutional neural network is a simple and elegant architecture with a 7.3% error rate. It has two versions: VGG16 and VGG19.

VGG16 is a 16-layer neural network, not counting the max pooling layer and the softmax layer. Hence, it is known as VGG16. VGG19 consists of 19 layers. A pre-trained model is available in Keras for both Theano and TensorFlow backends.

The key design consideration here is depth. Increases in the depth of the network were achieved by adding more convolution layers, and it was done due to the small 3 x 3 convolution filters in all the layers. The default input size of an image for this model is 224 x 224 x 3. The image is passed through a stack of convolution layers with a stride of 1 pixel and padding of 1. It uses 3 x 3 convolution throughout the network. Max pooling is done over a 2 x 2 pixel window with a stride of 2, then another stack of convolution layers followed by three fully connected layers. The first two fully connected layers have 4,096 neurons each, and the third fully connected layers are responsible for classification with 1,000 neurons. The final layer is a softmax layer. VGG16 uses a much smaller 3 x 3 convolution window, compared to AlexNet's much larger 11 x 11 convolution window. All hidden layers are built with the ReLU activation function. The architecture looks like this:

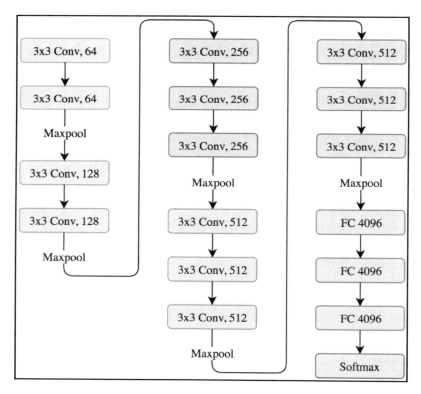

VGG16 network architecture

Due to the small 3 x 3 convolution filter, the depth of VGGNet is increased. The number of parameters in this network is approximately 140 million, mostly from the first fully connected layer. In latter-day architectures, fully connected layers of VGGNet are replaced with **global average pooling (GAP)** layers in order to minimize the number of parameters.

Another observation is that the number of filters increases as the image size decreases.

# VGG16 image classification code example

The Keras Applications module has pre-trained neural network models, along with its pre-trained weights trained on ImageNet. These models can be used directly for prediction, feature extraction, and fine-tuning:

```
#import VGG16 network model and other necessary libraries

from keras.applications.vgg16 import VGG16
from keras.preprocessing import image
from keras.applications.vgg16 import preprocess_input
import numpy as np

#Instantiate VGG16 and returns a vgg16 model instance
vgg16_model = VGG16(weights='imagenet', include_top=False)
#include_top: whether to include the 3 fully-connected layers at the top of
the network.
#This has to be True for classification and False for feature extraction.
Returns a model instance
#weights:'imagenet' means model is pre-training on ImageNet data.
model = VGG16(weights='imagenet', include_top=True)
model.summary()

#image file name to classify
image_path = 'jumping_dolphin.jpg'
#load the input image with keras helper utilities and resize the image.
#Default input size for this model is 224x224 pixels.
img = image.load_img(image_path, target_size=(224, 224))
#convert PIL (Python Image Library??) image to numpy array
x = image.img_to_array(img)
print (x.shape)

#image is now represented by a NumPy array of shape (224, 224, 3),
# but we need to expand the dimensions to be (1, 224, 224, 3) so we can
# pass it through the network -- we'll also preprocess the image by
# subtracting the mean RGB pixel intensity from the ImageNet dataset
```

```
#Finally, we can load our Keras network and classify the image:

x = np.expand_dims(x, axis=0)
print (x.shape)

preprocessed_image = preprocess_input(x)

preds = model.predict(preprocessed_image)
print('Prediction:', decode_predictions(preds, top=2)[0])
```

The first time it executes the preceding script, Keras will automatically download and cache the architecture weights to disk in the `~/.keras/models` directory. Subsequent runs will be faster.

# GoogLeNet architecture

In 2014, ILSVRC, Google published its own network known as **GoogLeNet**. Its performance is a little better than VGGNet; GoogLeNet's performance is 6.7% compared to VGGNet's performance of 7.3%. The main attractive feature of GoogLeNet is that it runs very fast due to the introduction of a new concept called **inception module**, thus reducing the number of parameters to only 5 million; that's 12 times less than AlexNet. It has lower memory use and lower power use too.

It has 22 layers, so it is a very deep network. Adding more layers increases the number of parameters and it is likely that the network overfits. There will be more computation, because a linear increase in filters results in a quadratic increase in computation. So, the designers use the inception module and GAP. The fully connected layer at the end of the network is replaced with a GAP layer because fully connected layers are generally prone to overfitting. GAP has no parameters to learn or optimize.

# Architecture insights

Instead of choosing a particular filter size as in the previous architectures, the GoogLeNet designers applied all the three filters of sizes 1 x 1, 3 x 3, and 5 x 5 on the same patch, with a 3 x 3 max pooling and concatenation into a single output vector.

The use of 1 x 1 convolutions decreases the dimensions wherever the computation is increased by the expensive 3 x 3 and 5 x 5 convolutions. 1 x 1 convolutions with the ReLU activation function are used before the expensive 3 x 3 and 5 x 5 convolutions.

In GoogLeNet, inception modules are stacked one over the other. This stacking allows us to modify each module without affecting the later layers. For example, you can increase or decrease the width of any layer:

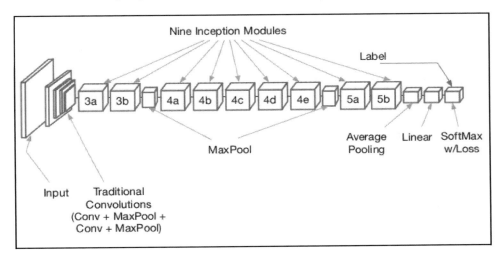

GoogLeNet architecture

Deep networks also suffer from the fear of what is known as the **vanishing gradient** problem during backpropagation. This is avoided by adding auxiliary classifiers to intermediate layers. Also, during training, the intermediate loss was added to the total loss with a discounted factor of 0.3.

Since fully connected layers are prone to overfitting, it is replaced with a GAP layer. Average pooling does not exclude use of dropout, a regularization method for overcoming overfitting in deep neural networks. GoogLeNet added a linear layer after 60, a GAP layer to help others swipe for their own classifier using transfer learning techniques.

# Inception module

The following image is an example of an inception module:

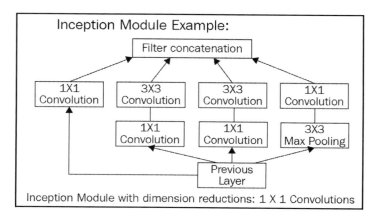

Inception Module Example:

Inception Module with dimension reductions: 1 X 1 Convolutions

# ResNet architecture

After a certain depth, adding additional layers to feed-forward convNets results in a higher training error and higher validation error. When adding layers, performance increases only up to a certain depth, and then it rapidly decreases. In the **ResNet (Residual Network)** paper, the authors argued that this underfitting is unlikely due to the vanishing gradient problem, because this happens even when using the batch normalization technique. Therefore, they have added a new concept called **residual block**. The ResNet team added connections that can skip layers:

ResNet uses standard convNet and adds connections that skip a few convolution layers at a time. Each bypass gives a residual block.

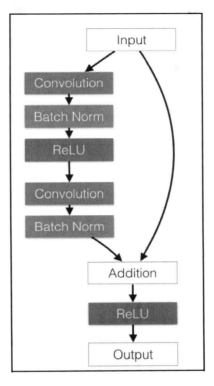

Residual block

In the 2015 ImageNet ILSVRC competition, the winner was ResNet from Microsoft, with an error rate of 3.57%. ResNet is a kind of VGG in the sense that the same structure is repeated again and again to make the network deeper. Unlike VGGNet, it has different depth variations, such as 34, 50, 101, and 152 layers. It has a whopping 152 layers compared to AlexNet 8, VGGNet's 19 layers, and GoogLeNet's 22 layers. The ResNet architecture is a stack of residual blocks. The main idea is to skip layers by adding connections to the neural network. Every residual block has 3 x 3 convolution layers. After the last conv layer, a GAP layer is added. There is only one fully connected layer to classify 1,000 classes. It has different depth varieties, such as 34, 50, 101, or 152 layers for the ImageNet dataset. For a deeper network, say more than 50 layers, it uses the **bottleneck** features concept to improve efficiency. No dropout is used in this network.

Other network architectures to be aware of include:

- Network in Network
- Beyond ResNet
- FractalNet, an ultra-deep neural network without residuals

# Summary

In this chapter, we learned about the different CNN architectures. These models are pre-trained existing models and differ in network architecture. Each of these networks is designed to solve a problem specific to its architecture. So, here we described their architectural differences.

We also understood how our own CNN architecture, as defined in the previous chapter, differs from these advanced ones.

In the next chapter, we will learn how these pre-trained models can be used for transfer learning.

# 5
# Transfer Learning

In the previous chapter, we learned that a CNN consists of several layers. We also studied different CNN architectures, tuned different hyperparameters, and identified values for stride, window size, and padding. Then we chose a correct loss function and optimized it. We trained this architecture with a large volume of images. So, the question here is, how do we make use of this knowledge with a different dataset? Instead of building a CNN architecture and training it from scratch, it is possible to take an existing pre-trained network and adapt it to a new and different dataset through a technique called **transfer learning**. We can do so through feature extraction and fine tuning.

Transfer learning is the process of copying knowledge from an already trained network to a new network to solve similar problems.

In this chapter, we will cover the following topics:

- Feature extraction approach
- Transfer learning example
- Multi-task learning

## Feature extraction approach

In a feature extraction approach, we train only the top level of the network; the rest of the network remains fixed. Consider a feature extraction approach when the new dataset is relatively small and similar to the original dataset. In such cases, the higher-level features learned from the original dataset should transfer well to the new dataset.

Consider a fine-tuning approach when the new dataset is large and similar to the original dataset. Altering the original weights should be safe because the network is unlikely to overfit the new, large dataset.

Let us consider a pre-trained convolutional neural network, as shown in the following diagram. Using this we can study how the transfer of knowledge can be used in different situations:

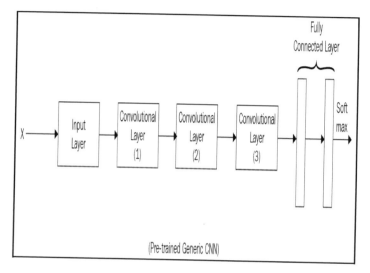

When should we use transfer learning? Transfer learning can be applied in the following situations, depending on:

- The size of the new (target) dataset
- Similarity between the original and target datasets

There are four main use cases:

- **Case 1**: New (target) dataset is small and is similar to the original training dataset
- **Case 2**: New (target) dataset is small but is different from the original training dataset
- **Case 3**: New (target) dataset is large and is similar to the original training dataset
- **Case 4**: New (target) dataset is large and is different from the original training dataset

Let us now walk through each case in detail in the following sections.

# Target dataset is small and is similar to the original training dataset

If the target dataset is small and similar to the original dataset:

- In this case, replace the last fully connected layer with a new fully connected layer that matches with the number of classes of the target dataset
- Initialize old weights with randomized weights
- Train the network to update the weights of the new, fully connected layer:

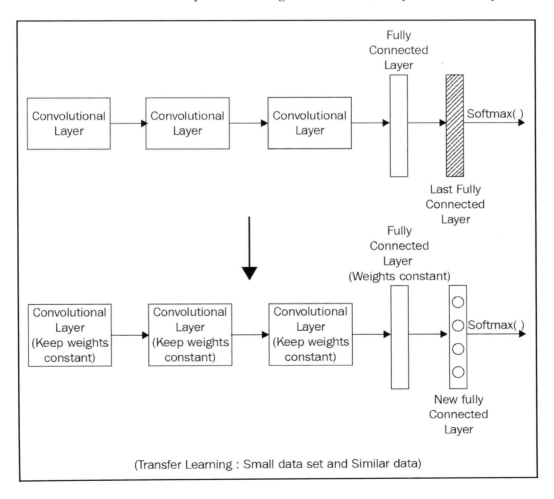

Transfer learning can be used as a strategy to avoid overfitting, especially when there is a small dataset.

# Target dataset is small but different from the original training dataset

If the target dataset is small but of a different type to the original – for example, the original dataset is dog images and the new (target) dataset is flower images – then do the following:

- Slice most of the initial layers of the network
- Add to the remaining pre-trained layers a new fully connected layer that matches the number of classes of the target dataset
- Randomize the weights of the new fully connected layer and freeze all the weights from the pre-trained network
- Train the network to update the weights of the new fully connected layer

Since the dataset is small, overfitting is still a concern here as well. To overcome this, we will keep the weights of the original pre-trained network the same and update only the weights of the new fully connected layer:

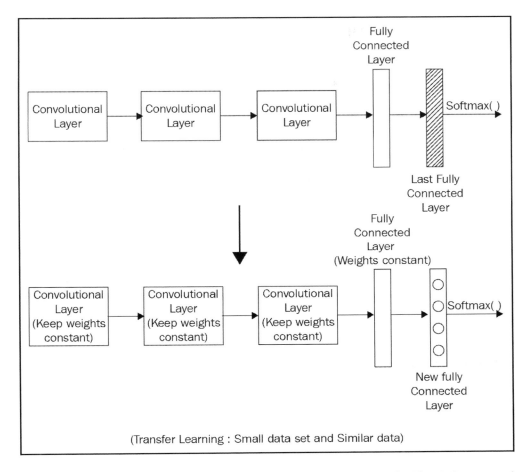

(Transfer Learning : Small data set and Similar data)

 Only fine tune the higher level portion of the network. This is because the beginning layers are designed to extract more generic features. In general, the first layer of a convolutional neural network is not specific to a dataset.

# Target dataset is large and similar to the original training dataset

Here we do not have an overfitting concern, as the dataset is large. So, in this case, we can retrain the entire network:

- Remove the last fully connected layer and replace it with a fully connected layer that matches the number of classes in the target dataset
- Randomly initialize the weights of this newly added, fully connected layer
- Initialize the rest of the weights with pre-trained weights
- Train the entire network:

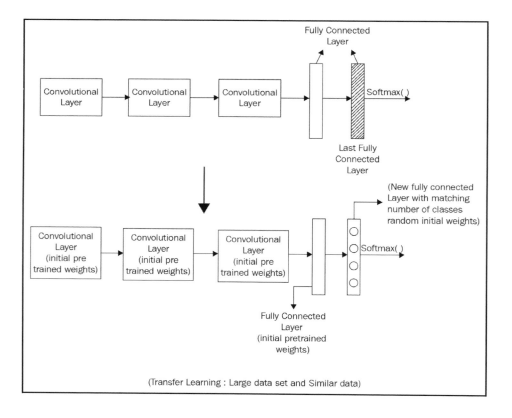

(Transfer Learning : Large data set and Similar data)

# Target dataset is large and different from the original training dataset

If the target dataset is large and different from the original:

- Remove the last fully connected layer and replace it with a fully connected layer that matches the number of classes in the target dataset
- Train the entire network from scratch with randomly initialized weights:

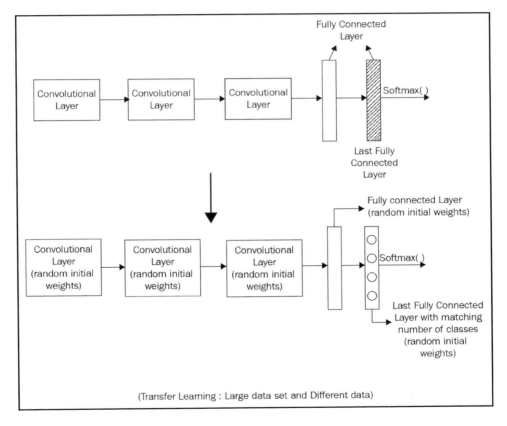

(Transfer Learning : Large data set and Different data)

The `Caffe` library has ModelZoo, where one can share network weights.

Consider training from scratch when the dataset is large and completely different from the original dataset. In this case, we have enough data to train from scratch without the fear of overfitting. However, even in this case, it might be beneficial to initialize the entire network with pre-trained weights and fine tune it on the new dataset.

# Transfer learning example

In this example, we will take a pre-trained VGGNet and use transfer learning to train a CNN classifier that predicts dog breeds, given a dog image. Keras contains many pre-trained models, along with the code that loads and visualizes them. Another is a flower dataset that can be downloaded here. The Dog breed dataset has 133 dog breed categories and 8,351 dog images. Download the Dog breed dataset here and copy it to your folder. VGGNet has 16 convolutional with pooling layers from beginning to end and three fully connected layers followed by a `softmax` function. Its main objective was to show how the depth of the network gives the best performance. It came from **Visual Geometric Group (VGG)** at Oxford. Their best performing network is VGG16. The Dog breed dataset is relatively small and has a little overlap with the `imageNet` dataset. So, we can remove the last fully connected layer after the convolutional layer and replace it with our own. The weights of the convolutional layer are kept constant. An input image is passed through the convolutional layer and stops at the 16th layer:

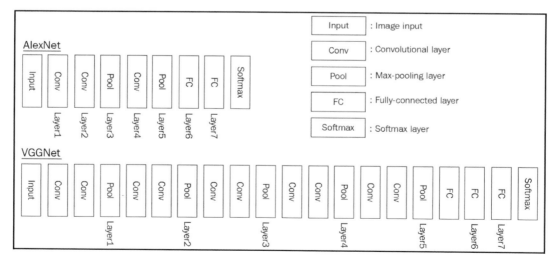

VGGNet Architecture

We will use the bottleneck features of a pre-trained VGG16 network – such a network has already learned features from the `imageNet` dataset. Because the `imageNet` dataset already contains a few images of dogs, the VGG16 network model has already learned key features for classification. Similarly, other pre-trained CNN architectures can also be considered as an exercise to solve other image classification tasks.

Download the `bottleneck_features` of VGG16 here, copy it to your own folder, and load it:

```
bottleneck_features = np.load('bottleneck_features/DogVGG16Data.npz')
train_vgg16 = bottleneck_features['train']
valid_vgg16 = bottleneck_features['valid']
test_vgg16 = bottleneck_features['test']
```

Now define the model architecture:

```
from keras.layers import GlobalAveragePooling2D

model = Sequential()
model.add(GlobalAveragePooling2D(input_shape=(7, 7, 512)))
model.add(Dense(133, activation='softmax'))
model.summary()

Layer (type)                      Output Shape           Param #
Connected to
===============================================================================
========================
globalaveragepooling2d_1 (Global  (None, 512)            0
globalaveragepooling2d_input_1[0]


dense_2 (Dense)                   (None, 133)            68229
globalaveragepooling2d_1[0][0]
===============================================================================
========================
Total params: 68,229
Trainable params: 68,229
Non-trainable params: 0
```

Compile the model and train it:

```
model.compile(loss='categorical_crossentropy', optimizer='rmsprop',
                    metrics=['accuracy'])
from keras.callbacks import ModelCheckpoint

# train the model
checkpointer = ModelCheckpoint(filepath='dogvgg16.weights.best.hdf5',
verbose=1,
                                    save_best_only=True)
model.fit(train_vgg16, train_targets, nb_epoch=20,
validation_data=(valid_vgg16, valid_targets),
        callbacks=[checkpointer], verbose=1, shuffle=True)
```

Load the model and calculate the classification accuracy on the test set:

```
# load the weights that yielded the best validation accuracy
model.load_weights('dogvgg16.weights.best.hdf5')
# get index of predicted dog breed for each image in test set
vgg16_predictions = [np.argmax(model.predict(np.expand_dims(feature,
axis=0)))
                    for feature in test_vgg16]

# report test accuracy
test_accuracy = 100*np.sum(np.array(vgg16_predictions)==
                                np.argmax(test_targets,
axis=1))/len(vgg16_predictions)
print('\nTest accuracy: %.4f%%' % test_accuracy)
```

# Multi-task learning

In multi-task learning, transfer learning happens to be from one pre-trained model to many tasks simultaneously. For example, in self-driving cars, the deep neural network detects traffic signs, pedestrians, and other cars in front at the same time. Speech recognition also benefits from multi-task learning.

# Summary

In a few specific cases, convolutional neural network architectures trained on images allow us to reuse learned features in a new network. The performance benefits of transferring features decrease the more dissimilar the base task and target task are. It is surprising to know that initializing a convolutional neural network with transferred features from almost any number of layers can produce a boost to generalization performance after fine-tuning to a new dataset.

# 6
# Autoencoders for CNN

In this chapter, we will cover the following topics:

- Introducing to Autoencoders
- Convolutional Autoencoder
- Applications of Autoencoders
- An example of compression

## Introducing to autoencoders

An autoencoder is a regular neural network, an unsupervised learning model that takes an input and produces the same input in the output layer. So, there is no associated label in the training data. Generally, an autoencoder consists of two parts:

- Encoder network
- Decoder network

It learns all the required features from unlabeled training data, which is known as lower dimensional feature representation. In the following figure, the input data ($x$) is passed through an encoder that produces a compressed representation of the input data. Mathematically, in the equation, $z = h(x)$, $z$ is a feature vector, and is usually a smaller dimension than $x$.

Then, we take these produced features from the input data and pass them through a decoder network to reconstruct the original data.

An encoder can be a fully connected neural network or a **convolutional neural network (CNN)**. A decoder also uses the same kind of network as an encoder. Here, we've explained and implemented the encoder and decoder function using ConvNet:

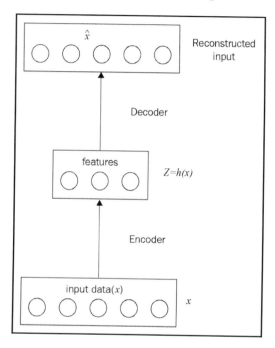

Loss function: $||x - x||^2$

 In this network, the size of the input and the output layers is the same.

# Convolutional autoencoder

A convolutional autoencoder is a neural network (a special case of an unsupervised learning model) that is trained to reproduce its input image in the output layer. An image is passed through an encoder, which is a ConvNet that produces a low-dimensional representation of the image. The decoder, which is another sample ConvNet, takes this compressed image and reconstructs the original image.

The encoder is used to compress the data and the decoder is used to reproduce the original image. Therefore, autoencoders may be used for data, compression. Compression logic is data-specific, meaning it is learned from data rather than predefined compression algorithms such as JPEG, MP3, and so on. Other applications of autoencoders can be image denoising (producing a cleaner image from a corrupted image), dimensionality reduction, and image search:

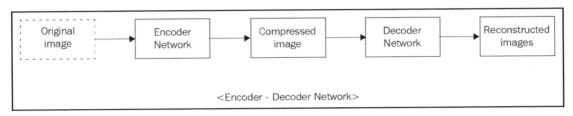

This differs from regular ConvNets or neural nets in the sense that the input size and the target size must be the same.

# Applications

Autoencoders are used for dimensionality reduction, or data compression, and image denoising. Dimensionality reduction, in turn, helps in improving runtime performance and consumes less memory. An image search can become highly efficient in low-dimension spaces.

# An example of compression

The Network architecture comprises of an encoder network, which is a typical convolutional pyramid. Each convolutional layer is followed by a max-pooling layer; this reduces the dimensions of the layers.

The decoder converts the input from a sparse representation to a wide reconstructed image. A schematic of the network is shown here:

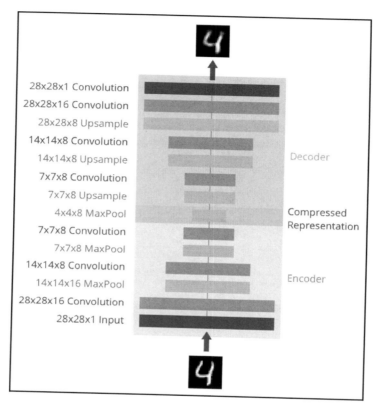

The encoder layer output image size is 4 x 4 x 8 = 128. The original image size was 28 x 28 x 1 = 784, so the compressed image vector is roughly 16% of the size of the original image.

Usually, you'll see transposed convolution layers used to increase the width and height of the layers. They work almost exactly the same as convolutional layers but in reverse. A stride in the input layer results in a larger stride in the transposed convolution layer. For example, if you have a 3 x 3 kernel, a 3 x 3 patch in the input layer will be reduced to one unit in a convolutional layer. Comparatively, one unit in the input layer will be expanded into a 3 x 3 path in a transposed convolution layer. The TensorFlow API provides us with an easy way to create the layers: `tf.nn.conv2d_transpose`, click here, https://www.tensorflow.org/api_docs/python/tf/nn/conv2d_transpose.

# Summary

We began this chapter with a short introduction to autoencoders, and we implemented the encoder and decoder function with the help of ConvNets.

We then moved to convolutional autoencoders and learned how they are different from regular ConvNets and neural nets.

We walked through the different applications of autoencoders, with an example, and saw how an autoencoder enhances the efficiency of image searches in low-dimension spaces.

In the next chapter, we will study object detection with CNNs and learn the difference between object detection and object classification.

# 7

# Object Detection and Instance Segmentation with CNN

Until now, in this book, we have been mostly using **convolutional neural networks** (**CNNs**) for classification. Classification classifies the whole image into one of the classes with respect to the entity having the maximum probability of detection in the image. But what if there is not one, but multiple entities of interest and we want to have the image associated with all of them? One way to do this is to use tags instead of classes, where these tags are all classes of the penultimate Softmax classification layer with probability above a given threshold. However, the probability of detection here varies widely by size and placement of entity, and from the following image, we can actually say, *How confident is the model that the identified entity is the one that is claimed?* What if we are very confident that there is an entity, say a dog, in the image, but its scale and position in the image is not as prominent as that of its owner, a *Person* entity? So, a *Multi-Class Tag* is a valid way but not the best for this purpose:

In this chapter, we will cover the following topics:

- The differences between object detection and image classification
- Traditional, non-CNN approaches for object detection
- Region-based CNN and its features
- Fast R-CNN
- Faster R-CNN
- Mask R-CNN

# The differences between object detection and image classification

Let's take another example. You are watching the movie *101 Dalmatians*, and you want to know how many Dalmatians you can actually count in a given movie scene from that movie. Image Classification could, at best, tell you that there is at least one dog or one *Dalmatian* (depending upon which level you have trained your classifier for), but not exactly how many of them there are.

Another issue with classification-based models is that they do not tell you where the identified entity in the image is. Many times, this is very important. Say, for example, you saw your neighbor's dog playing with him (*Person*) and his cat. You took a snap of them and wanted to extract the image of the dog from there to search on the web for its breed or similar dogs like it. The only problem here is that searching the whole image might not work, and without identifying individual objects from the image, you have to do the cut-extract-search job manually for this task, as shown in the following image:

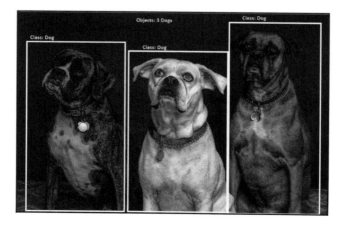

So, you essentially need a technique that not only identifies the entities in an image but also tells you their placement in the image. This is what is called **object detection**. Object detection gives you bounding boxes and class labels (along with the probability of detection) of all the entities identified in an image. The output of this system can be used to empower multiple advanced use cases that work on the specific class of the objects detected.

Take, for example, the Facial Recognition feature that you have in Facebook, Google Photos, and many other similar apps. In it, before you identify *who is* there in an image taken in at a party, you need to detect all the faces in that image; then you can pass these faces through your face recognition/classification module to get/classify their names. So, the Object nomenclature in object detection is not limited to linguistic entities but includes anything that has specific boundaries and enough data to train the system, as shown in the following image:

Now, if you want to find out how many of the guests present at your party were actually **enjoying** it, you can even run an object detection for **Smiling Faces** or a **Smile Detector**. There are very powerful and efficient trained models of object detectors available for most of the detectable human body parts (eye, face, upper body, and so on), popular human expressions (such as a smile), and many other general objects as well. So, the next time you use the **Smile Shutter** on your smartphone (a feature made to automatically click the image when most of the faces in the scene are detected as smiling), you know what is powering this feature.

# Why is object detection much more challenging than image classification?

From our understanding of CNN and image classification so far, let's try to understand how we can approach the object detection problem, and that should logically lead us to the discovery of the underlying complexity and challenges. Assume we are dealing with monochromatic images for simplicity.

Any object detection at a high level may be considered a combination of two tasks (we will refute this later):

- Getting the right bounding boxes (or as many of them to filter later)
- Classifying the object in that bounding box (while returning the classification effectiveness for filtering)

So, object detection not only has to cater to all the challenges of image classification (second objective), but also faces new challenges of finding the right, or as many as possible, bounding boxes. As we already know how to use CNNs for the purpose of image classification, and the associated challenges, we can now concentrate on our first task and explore how effective (classification accuracy) and efficient (computational complexity) our approach is—or rather how challenging this task is going to be.

So, we start with randomly generating bounding boxes from the image. Even if we do not worry about the computational load of generating so many candidate boxes, technically termed as **Region Proposals** (regions that we send as proposals for classifying objects), we still need to have some mechanism for finding the best values for the following parameters:

- Starting (or center) coordinates to extract/draw the candidate bounding box
- Length of the candidate bounding box
- Width of the candidate bounding box
- Stride across each axis (distance from one starting location to another in the $x$-horizontal axis and $y$-vertical axis)

Let's assume that we can generate such an algorithm that can give us the most optimal value of these parameters. Still, will one value for these parameters work in most of the cases, or in fact, in some general cases? From our experience, we know that each object will have a different scale, so we know that one fixed value for $L$ and $W$ for these boxes will not work. Also, we can understand that the same object, say Dog, may be present in varying proportions/scales and positions in different images, as in some of our earlier examples. So this confirms our belief that we need boxes of not only different scales but also different sizes.

Let's assume that, correcting from the previous analogy, we want to extract $N$ number of candidate boxes per starting coordinate in the image, where $N$ encompasses most of the sizes/scales that may fit our classification problem. Although that seems to be a rather challenging job in itself, let's assume we have that magic number and it is far from a combination of *L[1,l-image] x W[1,w-image]* (all combinations of $L$ and $W$ where length is a set of all integers between 1 and the length of the actual image and breadth is from 1 to the breadth of the image); that will lead us to *l*w* boxes per coordinate:

Then, another question is about how many starting coordinates we need to visit in our image from where we will extract these $N$ boxes each, or the Stride. Using a very big stride will lead us to extract sub-images in themselves, instead of a single homogeneous object that can be classified effectively and used for the purpose of achieving some of the objectives in our earlier examples. Conversely, too short a stride (say, 1 pixel in each direction) may mean a lot of candidate boxes.

From the preceding illustration, we can understand that even after hypothetically relaxing most of the constraints, we are nowhere close to making a system that we can fit in our Smartphones to detect smiling selfies or even bright faces in real time (even after an hour in fact). Nor can it have our robots and self-driving cars identify objects as they move (and navigate their way by avoiding them). This intuition should help us appreciate the advancements in the field of object detection and why it is such an impactful area of work.

# Traditional, nonCNN approaches to object detection

Libraries such as OpenCV and some others saw rapid inclusion in the software bundles for Smartphones, Robotic projects, and many others, to provide detection capabilities of specific objects (face, smile, and so on), and Computer Vision like benefits, though with some constraints even before the prolific adoption of CNN.

CNN-based research in this area of object detection and Instance Segmentation provided many advancements and performance enhancements to this field, not only enabling large-scale deployment of these systems but also opening avenues for many new solutions. But before we plan to jump into CNN based advancements, it will be a good idea to understand how the challenges cited in the earlier section were answered to make object detection possible in the first place (even with all the constraints), and then we will logically start our discussion about the different researchers and the application of CNN to solve other problems that still persist with the use of traditional approaches.

# Haar features, cascading classifiers, and the Viola-Jones algorithm

Unlike CNN, or the deepest learning for that matter, which is known for its capability of generating higher conceptual features automatically, which in-turn gives a major boost to the classifier, in case of traditional machine learning applications, such features need to be hand crafted by SMEs.

As we may also understand from our experience working on CPU-based machine learning classifiers, their performance is affected by high dimensionality in data and the availability of too many features to apply to the model, especially with some of the very popular and sophisticated classifiers such as **Support Vector Machines** (**SVM**), which used to be considered state-of-the-art until some time ago.

In this section, we will understand some of the innovative ideas drawing inspirations from different fields of science and mathematics that led to the resolution of some of the cited challenges above, to fructify the concept of real-time object detection in non-CNN systems.

# Haar Features

Haar or Haar-like features are formations of rectangles with varying pixel density. Haar features sum up the pixel intensity in the adjacent rectangular regions at specific locations in the detection region. Based on the difference between the sums of pixel intensities across regions, they categorize the different subsections of the image.

Haar-like features have their name attributed to the mathematics term of Haar wavelet, which is a sequence of rescaled square-shaped functions that together form a wavelet family or basis.

Because Haar-like features work on the difference between pixel intensities across regions, they work best with monochrome images. This is also the reason the images used earlier and in also this section are monochrome for better intuition.

These categories can be grouped into three major groups, as follows:

- Two rectangle features
- Three rectangle features
- Four rectangle features

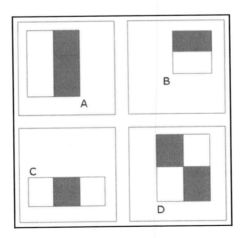

Haar-like Features

With some easy tricks, the computation of varying intensities across the image becomes very efficient and can be processed at a very high rate in real time.

# Cascading classifiers

Even if we can extract Haar features from a particular region very quickly, it does not solve the problem of extracting such features from a lot of different places in the image; this is where the concept of cascading features comes in to help. It was observed that only 1 in 10,000 sub-regions turns positive for faces in classification, but we have to extract all features and run the whole classifier across all regions. Further, it was observed that by using just a few of the features (two in the first layer of the cascade), the classifier could eliminate a very high proportion of the regions (50% in the first region of the cascade). Also, if the sample consists of just these reduced region samples, then only slightly more features (10 features in the second layer of the cascade) are required for a classifier that can weed out a lot more cases, and so on. So we do classification in layers, starting with a classifier that requires very low computational power to weed out most of the subregions, gradually increasing the computation load required for the remaining subset, and so on.

# The Viola-Jones algorithm

In 2001, Paul Viola and Michael Jones proposed a solution that could work well to answer some of the preceding challenges, but with some constraints. Though it is an almost two decades old algorithm, some of the most popular computer vision software to date, or at least till recently, used to embed it in some form or another. This fact makes it very important to understand this very simple, yet powerful, algorithm before we move on to CNN-based approaches for Region Proposal.

OpenCV, one of the most popular software libraries for computer vision, uses cascading classifiers as the predominant mode for object detection, and Haar-featuring-like Cascade classifier is very popular with OpenCV. A lot of pretrained Haar classifiers are available for this for multiple types of general objects.

This algorithm is not only capable of delivering detections with high **TPRs (True Positive Rates)** and low **FPRs (False Positive Rates)**, it can also work in real time (process at least two frames per second).

High TPR combined with Low FPR is a very important criterion for determining the robustness of an algorithm.

The constraints of their proposed algorithm were the following:

- It could work only for detecting, not recognizing faces (they proposed the algorithm for faces, though the same could be used for many other objects).
- The faces had to be present in the image as a frontal view. No other view could be detected.

At the heart of this algorithm are the Haar (like) Features and Cascading Classifiers. Haar Features are described later in a subsection. The Viola-Jones algorithm uses a subset of Haar features to determine general features on a face such as:

- Eyes (determined by a two-rectangle feature (horizontal), with a dark horizontal rectangle above the eye forming the brow, followed by a lighter rectangle below)
- Nose (three-rectangle feature (vertical), with the nose as the center light rectangle and one darker rectangle on either side on the nose, forming the temple), and so on

These fast-to-extract features can then be used to make a classifier to detect (distinguish) faces (from non-faces).

Haar features, with some tricks, are very fast to compute.

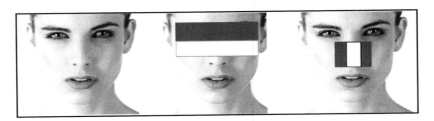
Viola-Jones algorithm and Haar-like Features for detecting faces

These Haar-like features are then used in the cascading classifiers to expedite the detection problem without losing the robustness of detection.

The Haar Features and cascading classifiers thus led to some of the very robust, effective, and fast individual object detectors of the previous generation. But still, the training of these cascades for a new object was very time consuming, and they had a lot of constraints, as mentioned before. That is where the new generation CNN-based object detectors come to the rescue.

In this chapter, we have covered only the basis of Haar-Cascades or Haar features (in the non-CNN category) as they remained predominant for a long time and were the basis of many new types. Readers are encouraged to also explore some of the later and much effective SIFT and HOG-based features/cascades (associated papers are given in the *References* section).

# R-CNN – Regions with CNN features

In the 'Why is object detection much more challenging than image classification?' section, we used a non-CNN method to draw region proposals and CNN for classification, and we realized that this is not going to work well because the regions generated and fed into CNN were not optimal. R-CNN or regions with CNN features, as the name suggests, flips that example completely and use CNN to generate features that are classified using a (non-CNN) technique called **SVM (Support Vector Machines)**

R-CNN uses the sliding window method (much like we discussed earlier, taking some *L x W* and stride) to generate around 2,000 regions of interest, and then it converts them into features for classification using CNN. Remember what we discussed in the transfer learning chapter—the last flattened layer (before the classification or softmax layer) can be extracted to transfer learning from models trained on generalistic data, and further train them (often requiring much less data as compared to a model with similar performance that has been trained from scratch using domain-specific data) to model domain-specific models. R-CNNs also use a similar mechanism to improve their effectiveness on specific object detection:

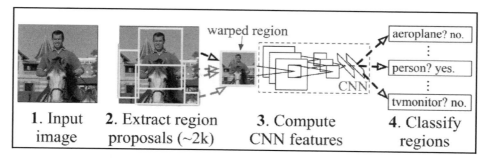

R-CNN – Working

The original paper on R-CNN claims that on a PASCAL VOC 2012 dataset, it has improved the **mean average precision (mAP)** by more than 30% relative to the previous best result on that data while achieving a mAP of 53.3%.

We saw very high precision figures for the image classification exercise (using CNN) over the ImageNet data. Do not use that figure with the comparison statistics given here, as not only are the datasets used different (and hence not comparable), but also the tasks in hand (classification versus object detection) are quite different, and object detection is much more challenging a task than image classification.

PASCAL **VOC (Visual Object Challenge)**: Every area of research requires some sort of standardized dataset and standard KPIs to compare results across different studies and algorithms. Imagenet, the dataset we used for image classification, cannot be used as a standardized dataset for object detection, as object-detection requires (train, test, and validation set) data labeled with not only the object class but also its position. ImageNet does not provide this. Therefore, in most object detection studies, we may see the use of a standardized object-detection dataset, such as PASCAL VOC. The PASCAL VOC dataset has 4 variants so far, VOC2007, VOC2009, VOC2010, and VOC2012. VOC2012 is the latest (and richest) of them all.

Another place we stumbled at was the differing scales (and location) of the regions of interest, *recognition using region*. This is what is called the **localization** challenge; it is solved in R-CNN by using a varying range of receptive fields, starting from as high a region with 195 x 195 pixels and 32 x 32 strides, to lesser downwards.

This approach is called **recognition using region**.

Wait a minute! Does that ring a bell? We said that we will use CNN to generate features from this region, but CNN uses a constant-size input to produce a fixed-size flattened layer. We do require fixed-size features (flattened vector size) as input to our SVMs, but here the input region size is changing. So how does that work? R-CNN uses a popular technique called **Affine Image Warping** to compute a fixed-size CNN input from each region proposal, regardless of the region's shape.

In geometry, an affine transformation is the name given to a transformation function between affine spaces that preserves points, straight lines, and planes. Affine spaces are structures that generalize the properties of Euclidian spaces while preserving only the properties related to parallelism and respective scale.

Besides the challenges that we have covered, there exists another challenge that is worth mentioning. The candidate regions that we generated in the first step (on which we performed classification in the second step) were not very accurate, or they were lacking tight boundaries around the object identified. So we include a third stage in this method, which improves the accuracy of the bounding boxes by running a regression function (called **bounding-box regressors**) to identify the boundaries of separation.

R-CNN proved to be very successful when compared to the earlier end-to-end non-CNN approaches. But it uses CNN only for converting regions to features. As we understand, CNNs are very powerful for image classifications as well, but because our CNN will work only on input region images and not on flattened region features, we cannot use it here directly. In the next section, we will see how to overcome this obstacle.

R-CNN is very important to cover from the perspective of understanding the background use of CNN in object detection as it has been a giant leap from all non-CNN-based approaches. But because of further improvements in CNN-based object detection, as we will discuss next, R-CNN is not actively worked upon now and the code is not maintained any longer.

# Fast R-CNN – fast region-based CNN

Fast R-CNN, or Fast Region-based CNN method, is an improvement over the previously covered R-CNN. To be precise about the improvement statistics, as compared to R-CNN, it is:

- 9x faster in training
- 213x faster at scoring/servicing/testing (0.3s per image processing), ignoring the time spent on region proposals
- Has higher mAP of 66% on the PASCAL VOC 2012 dataset

Where R-CNN uses a smaller (five-layer) CNN, Fast R-CNN uses the deeper VGG16 network, which accounts for its improved accuracy. Also, R-CNN is slow because it performs a ConvNet forward pass for each object proposal without sharing computation:

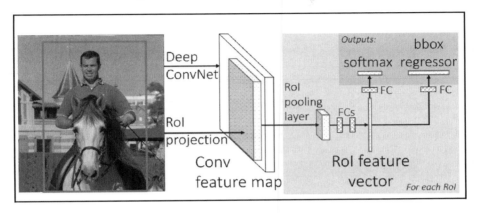

Fast R-CNN: Working

In Fast R-CNN, the deep VGG16 CNN provides essential computations for all the stages, namely:

- **Region of Interest (RoI)** computation
- Classification Objects (or background) for the region contents
- Regression for enhancing the bounding box

The input to the CNN, in this case, is not raw (candidate) regions from the image, but the (complete) actual image itself; the output is not the last flattened layer but the convolution (map) layer before that. From the so-generated convolution map, a the RoI pooling layer (a variant of max-pooling) is used to generate the flattened fixed-length RoI corresponding to each object proposal are generated, which are then passed through some **fully connected (FC)** layers.

The RoI pooling is a variant of max pooling (that we used in our initial chapters in this book), in which output size is fixed and input rectangle is a parameter.

The RoI pooling layer uses max pooling to convert the features inside any valid region of interest into a small feature map with a fixed spatial extent.

The output from the penultimate FC layer is then used for both:

- Classification (SoftMax layer) with as many classes as object proposals, +1 additional class for the background (none of the classes found in the region)
- Sets of regressors that produce the four numbers (two numbers denoting the x, y coordinates of the upper-left corner for the box for that object, and the next two numbers corresponding to the height and width of that object found in that region) for each object-proposal that is required to make bounding boxes precise for that particular object

The result achieved with Fast R-CNN is great. What is even greater is the use of a powerful CNN network to provide very effective features for all three challenges that we need to overcome. But there are still some drawbacks, and there is scope for further improvements as we will understand in our next section on Faster R-CNN.

# Faster R-CNN – faster region proposal network-based CNN

We saw in the earlier section that Fast R-CNN brought down the time required for scoring (testing) images drastically, but the reduction ignored the time required for generating Region Proposals, which use a separate mechanism (though pulling from the convolution map from CNN) and continue proving a bottleneck. Also, we observed that though all three challenges were resolved using the common features from convolution-map in Fast R-CNN, they were using different mechanisms/models.

Faster R-CNN improves upon these drawbacks and proposes the concept of **Region Proposal Networks** (**RPNs**), bringing down the scoring (testing) time to 0.2 seconds per image, even including time for Region Proposals.

 Fast R-CNN was doing the scoring (testing) in 0.3 seconds per image, that too excluding the time required for the process equivalent to Region Proposal.

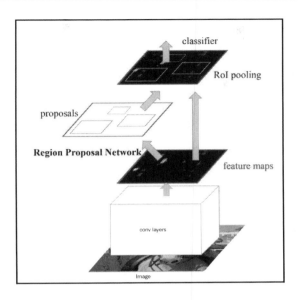

Faster R-CNN: Working - The Region Proposal Networking acting as Attention Mechanism

As shown in the earlier figure, a VGG16 (or another) CNN works directly on the image, producing a convolutional map (similar to what was done in Fast R-CNN). Things differ from here, where now there are two branches, one feeding into the RPN and the other into the detection Network. This is again an extension of the same CNN for prediction, leading to a **Fully Convolutional Network** (**FCN**). The RPN acts as an Attention Mechanism and also shares full-image convolutional features with the detection network. Also, now because all the parts in the network can use efficient GPU-based computation, it thus reduces the overall time required:

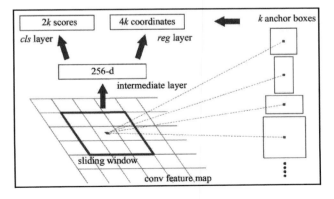

Faster R-CNN: Working - The Region Proposal Networking acting as Attention Mechanism

For a greater understanding of the Attention Mechanism, refer to the chapter on Attention Mechanisms for CNN in this book.

The RPN works in a sliding window mechanism, where a window slides (much like CNN filters) across the last convolution map from the shared convolutional layer. With each slide, the sliding window produces $k$ ($k=N_{Scale} \times N_{Size}$) number of Anchor Boxes (similar to Candidate Boxes), where $N_{Scale}$ is the number of (pyramid like) scales per *size* of the $N_{Size}$ sized (aspect ratio) box extracted from the center of the sliding window, much like the following figure.

The RPN leads into a flattened, FC layer. This, in turn, leads into two networks, one for predicting the four numbers for each of the $k$ boxes (determining the coordinates, length and width of the box as in Fast R-CNN), and another into a binomial classification model that determines the objectness or probability of finding any of the given objects in that box. The output from the RPN leads into the detection network, which detects which particular class of object is in each of the k boxes given the position of the box and its objectness.

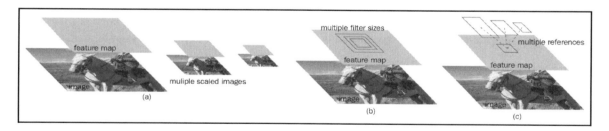

Faster R-CNN: Working - extracting different scales and sizes

One problem in this architecture is the training of the two networks, namely the Region Proposal and detection network. We learned that CNN is trained using backpropagating across all layers while reducing the losses layers with every iteration. But because of the split into two different networks, we could at a time backpropagate across only one network. To resolve this issue, the training is done iteratively across each network, while keeping the weights of the other network constant. This helps in converging both the networks quickly.

An important feature of the RPN architecture is that it has translation invariance with respect to both the functions, one that is producing the anchors, and another that is producing the attributes (its coordinate and objectness) for the anchors. Because of translation invariance, a reverse operation, or producing the portion of the image given a vector map of an anchor map is feasible.

 Owing to Translational Invariance, we can move in either direction in a CNN, that is from image to (region) proposals, and from the proposals to the corresponding portion of the image.

# Mask R-CNN – Instance segmentation with CNN

Faster R-CNN is state-of-the-art stuff in object detection today. But there are problems overlapping the area of object detection that Faster R-CNN cannot solve effectively, which is where Mask R-CNN, an evolution of Faster R-CNN can help.

This section introduces the concept of instance segmentation, which is a combination of the standard object detection problem as described in this chapter, and the challenge of semantic segmentation.

 In semantic segmentation, as applied to images, the goal is to classify each pixel into a fixed set of categories without differentiating object instances.

Remember our example of counting the number of dogs in the image in the intuition section? We were able to count the number of dogs easily, because they were very much apart, with no overlap, so essentially just counting the number of objects did the job. Now, take the following image, for instance, and count the number of tomatoes using object detection. It will be a daunting task because the Bounding Boxes will have so much of an overlap that it will be difficult to distinguish the Instances of tomatoes from the boxes.

So, essentially, we need to go further, beyond bounding boxes and into pixels to get that level separation and identification. Like we use to classify bounding boxes with object names in object detection, in Instance Segment, we segment/ classify, each pixel with not only the specific object name but also the object-instance.

The object detection and Instance Segmentation could be treated as two different tasks, one logically leading to another, much like we discovered the tasks of finding Region Proposals and Classification in the case of object detection. But as in the case of object detection, and especially with techniques like Fast/Faster R-CNN, we discovered that it would be much effective if we have a mechanism to do them simultaneously, while also utilizing much of the computation and network to do so, to make the tasks seamless.

Instance Segmentation – Intuition

Mask R-CNN is an extension of Faster R-CNN covered in the earlier network, and uses all the techniques used in Faster R-CNN, with one addition—an additional path in the network to generate a Segmentation Mask (or Object Mask) for each detected Object Instance in parallel. Also, because of this approach of using most of the existing network, it adds only a minimal overhead to the entire processing and has a scoring (test) time almost equivalent to that of Faster R-CNN. It has one of the best accuracies across all single-model solutions as applied to the COCO2016 challenge (using the COCO2015 dataset).

Like, PASCAL VOC, COCO is another large-scale standard (series of) dataset (from Microsoft). Besides object detection, COCO is also used for segmentation and captioning. COCO is more extensive than many other datasets and much of the recent comparison on object detection is done on this for comparison purposes. The COCO dataset comes in three variants, namely COCO 2014, COCO 2015, and COCO 2017.

In Mask R-CNN, besides having the two branches that generate the objectness and localization for each anchor box or RoI, there also exists a third FCN that takes in the RoI and predicts a segmentation mask in a pixel-to-pixel manner for the given anchor box.

But there still remain some challenges. Though Faster R-CNN does demonstrate transformational invariance (that is, we could trace from the convolutional map of the RPN to the pixel map of the actual image), the convolutional map has a different structure from that of the actual image pixels. So, there is no pixel-to-pixel alignment between network inputs and outputs, which is important for our purpose of providing pixel-to-pixel masking using this network. To solve this challenge, Mask R-CNN uses a quantization-free layer (named RoIAlign in the original paper) that helps align the exact spatial locations. This layer not only provides exact alignment but also helps in improving the accuracy to a great extent, because of which Mask R-CNN is able to outperform many other networks:

Mask R-CNN – Instance Segmentation Mask (illustrative output)

The concept of instance segmentation is very powerful and can lead to realizing a lot of very impactful use cases that were not possible with object detection alone.

We can even use instance segmentation to estimate human poses in the same framework and eliminate them.

# Instance segmentation in code

It's now time to put the things that we've learned into practice. We'll use the COCO dataset and its API for the data, and use Facebook Research's Detectron project (link in References), which provides the Python implementation of many of the previously discussed techniques under an Apache 2.0 license. The code works with Python2 and Caffe2, so we'll need a virtual environment with the given configuration.

# Creating the environment

The virtual environment, with Caffe2 installation, can be created as per the `caffe2` installation instructions on the Caffe2 repository link in the *References* Section. Next, we will install the dependencies.

## Installing Python dependencies (Python2 environment)

We can install the Python dependencies as shown in the following code block:

Python 2X and Python 3X are two different flavors of Python (or more precisely CPython), and not a conventional upgrade of version, therefore the libraries for one variant might not be compatible with another. Use Python 2X for this section.

*When we refer to the (interpreted) programming language Python, we need to refer to it with the specific interpreter (since it is an interpreted language as opposed to a compiled one like Java). The interpreter that we implicitly refer to as the Python interpreter (like the one you download from Python.org or the one that comes bundled with Anaconda) is technically called CPython, on which is the default byte-code interpreter of Python, which is written in C. But there are other Python interpreters also like Jython (build on Java), PyPy (written in Python itself - not so intuitive, right?), IronPython (.NET implementation of Python).*

```
pip install numpy>=1.13 pyyaml>=3.12 matplotlib opencv-python>=3.2
setuptools Cython mock scipy
```

# Downloading and installing the COCO API and detectron library (OS shell commands)

We will then download and install the Python dependencies as shown in the following code block:

```
# COCO API download and install
# COCOAPI=/path/to/clone/cocoapi
git clone https://github.com/cocodataset/cocoapi.git $COCOAPI
cd $COCOAPI/PythonAPI
make install

# Detectron library download and install
# DETECTRON=/path/to/clone/detectron
git clone https://github.com/facebookresearch/detectron $DETECTRON
cd $DETECTRON/lib && make
```

Alternatively, we can download and use the Docker image of the environment (requires Nvidia GPU support):

```
# DOCKER image build
cd $DETECTRON/docker docker build -t detectron:c2-cuda9-cudnn7.
nvidia-docker run --rm -it detectron:c2-cuda9-cudnn7 python2
tests/test_batch_permutation_op.py
```

# Preparing the COCO dataset folder structure

Now we will see the code to prepare the COCO dataset folder structure as follows:

```
# We need the following Folder structure: coco [coco_train2014,
coco_val2014, annotations]
mkdir -p $DETECTRON/lib/datasets/data/coco
ln -s /path/to/coco_train2014 $DETECTRON/lib/datasets/data/coco/
ln -s /path/to/coco_val2014 $DETECTRON/lib/datasets/data/coco/
ln -s /path/to/json/annotations
$DETECTRON/lib/datasets/data/coco/annotations
```

# Running the pre-trained model on the COCO dataset

We can now implement the pre-trained model on the COCO dataset as shown in the following code snippet:

```
python2 tools/test_net.py \
    --cfg configs/12_2017_baselines/e2e_mask_rcnn_R-101-FPN_2x.yaml \
    TEST.WEIGHTS
https://s3-us-west-2.amazonaws.com/detectron/35861858/12_2017_baselines/e2e
_mask_rcnn_R-101-
FPN_2x.yaml.02_32_51.SgT4y1cO/output/train/coco_2014_train:coco_2014_valmin
usminival/generalized_rcnn/model_final.pkl \
    NUM_GPUS 1
```

# References

1. Paul Viola and Michael Jones, Rapid object detection using a boosted cascade of simple features, *Conference on Computer Vision and Pattern Recognition*, 2001.

2. Paul Viola and Michael Jones, Robust Real-time object detection, *International Journal of Computer Vision*, 2001.

3. Itseez2015opencv, OpenCV, *Open Source Computer Vision Library*, Itseez, 2015.

4. Ross B. Girshick, Jeff Donahue, Trevor Darrell, Jitendra Malik, *Rich feature hierarchies for accurate object detection and semantic segmentation*, CoRR, arXiv:1311.2524, 2013.

5. Ross Girshick, Jeff Donahue, Trevor Darrell, Jitendra Malik, *Rich feature hierarchies for accurate object detection and semantic segmentation*, Computer Vision and Pattern Recognition, 2014.

6. M. Everingham, L. VanGool, C. K. I. Williams, J. Winn, A. Zisserman, *The PASCAL Visual Object Classes Challenge 2012*, VOC2012, Results.

7. D. Lowe. *Distinctive image features from scale-invariant keypoints*, IJCV, 2004.

8. N. Dalal and B. Triggs. *Histograms of oriented gradients for human detection.* In CVPR, 2005.

9. Ross B. Girshick, Fast R-CNN, CoRR, arXiv:1504.08083, 2015.

10. Rbgirshick, fast-rcnn, GitHub, `https://github.com/rbgirshick/fast-rcnn`, Feb-2018.

11. Shaoqing Ren, Kaiming He, Ross B. Girshick, Jian Sun, Faster R-CNN: *Towards Real-Time Object Detection with Region Proposal Networks*, CoRR, arXiv:1506.01497, 2015.

12. Shaoqing Ren and Kaiming He and Ross Girshick and Jian Sun, Faster R-CNN: *Towards Real-Time Object Detection with Region Proposal Networks*, Advances in **Neural Information Processing Systems (NIPS)**, 2015.

13. Rbgirshick, py-faster-rcnn, GitHub, `https://github.com/rbgirshick/py-faster-rcnn`, Feb-2018.

14. Ross Girshick, Ilija Radosavovic, Georgia Gkioxari, Piotr Dollar, Kaiming He, Detectron, GitHub, `https://github.com/facebookresearch/Detectron`, Feb-2018.

15. Tsung-Yi Lin, Michael Maire, Serge J. Belongie, Lubomir D. Bourdev, Ross B. Girshick, James Hays, Pietro Perona, Deva Ramanan, Piotr Dollar, C. Lawrence Zitnick, *Microsoft COCO: Common Objects in Context*, CoRR, arXiv:1405.0312, 2014.

16. Kaiming He, Georgia Gkioxari, Piotr Dollar, Ross B. Girshick, Mask R-CNN, CoRR, arXiv:1703.06870, 2017.

17. Liang-Chieh Chen, Alexander Hermans, George Papandreou, Florian Schroff, Peng Wang, Hartwig Adam, MaskLab: *Instance Segmentation by Refining Object Detection with Semantic and Direction Features*, CoRR, arXiv:1712.04837, 2017.

18. Anurag Arnab, Philip H. S. Torr, *Pixelwise Instance Segmentation with a Dynamically Instantiated Network*, CoRR, arXiv:1704.02386, 2017.

19. Matterport, Mask_RCNN, GitHub, `https://github.com/matterport/Mask_RCNN`, Feb-2018.

20. CharlesShang, FastMaskRCNN, GitHub, `https://github.com/CharlesShang/FastMaskRCNN`, Feb-2018.

21. Caffe2, Caffe2, GitHub, `https://github.com/caffe2/caffe2`, Feb-2018.

# Summary

In this chapter, we started from the very simple intuition behind the task of object detection and then proceeded to very advanced concepts, such as Instance Segmentation, which is a contemporary research area. Object detection is at the heart of a lot of innovation in the field of Retail, Media, Social Media, Mobility, and Security; there is a lot of potential for using these technologies to create very impactful and profitable features for both enterprise and social consumption.

From the Algorithms perspective, this chapter started with the legendary Viola-Jones algorithm and its underlying mechanisms, such as Haar Features and Cascading Classifiers. Using that intuition, we started exploring the world of CNN for object detection with algorithms, such as R-CNN, Fast R-CNN, up to the very state-of-the-art Faster R-CNN.

In this chapter, we also laid the foundations and introduced a very recent and impactful field of research called **instance segmentation**. We also covered some state-of-the-art Deep CNNs based on methods, such as Mask R-CNN, for easy and performant implementation of instance segmentation.

# 8

# GAN: Generating New Images with CNN

Generally, a neural network needs labeled examples to learn effectively. Unsupervised learning approaches to learn from unlabeled data have not worked very well. A **generative adversarial network**, or simply a **GAN**, is part of an unsupervised learning approach but based on differentiable generator networks. GANs were first invented by Ian Goodfellow and others in 2014. Since then they have become extremely popular. This is based on game theory and has two players or networks: a generator network and b) a discriminator network, both competing against each other. This dual network game theory-based approach vastly improved the process of learning from unlabeled data. The generator network produces fake data and passes it to a discriminator. The discriminator network also sees real data and predicts whether the data it receives is fake or real. So, the generator is trained so that it can easily produce data that is very close to real data in order to fool the discriminator network. The discriminator network is trained to classify which data is real and which data is fake. So, eventually, a generator network learns to produce data that is very, very close to real data. GANs are going to be widely popular in the music and arts domains.

 According to Goodfellow, "*You can think of generative models as giving Artificial Intelligence a form of imagination.*"

The following are a couple of examples of GANs:

- Pix2pix
- CycleGAN

# Pix2pix - Image-to-Image translation GAN

This network uses a **conditional generative adversarial network (cGAN)** to learn mapping from the input and output of an image. Some of the examples that can be done from the original paper are as follows:

Pix2pix examples of cGANs

In the handbags example, the network learns how to color a black and white image. Here, the training dataset has the input image in black and white and the target image is the color version.

# CycleGAN

CycleGAN is also an image-to-image translator but without input/output pairs. For example, to generate photos from paintings, convert a horse image into a zebra image:

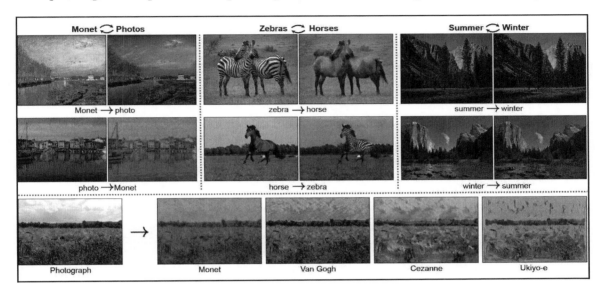

> In a discriminator network, use of dropout is important. Otherwise, it may produce a poor result.

The generator network takes random noise as input and produces a realistic image as output. Running a generator network for different kinds of random noise produces different types of realistic images. The second network, which is known as the **discriminator network**, is very similar to a regular neural net classifier. This network is trained on real images, although training a GAN is quite different from a supervised training method. In supervised training, each image is labeled first before being shown to the model. For example, if the input is a dog image, we tell the model this is a dog. In case of a generative model, we show the model a lot of images and ask it to make more such similar images from the same probability distribution. Actually, the second discriminator network helps the generator network to achieve this.

The discriminator outputs the probability that the image is real or fake from the generator network. In other words, it tries to assign a probability close to 1 for a real image and a probability close to 0 for fake images. Meanwhile, the generator does the opposite. It is trained to output images that will have a probability close to 1 by the discriminator. Over time, the generator produces more realistic images and fools the discriminator:

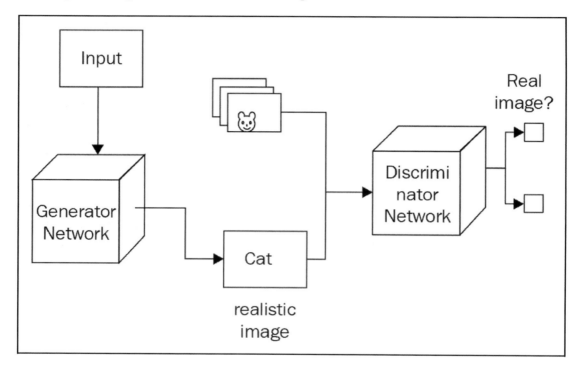

# Training a GAN model

Most machine learning models explained in earlier chapters are based on optimization, that is, we minimize the cost function over its parameter space. GANs are different because of two networks: the generator G and the discriminator D. Each has its own cost. An easy way to visualize GAN is the cost of the discriminator is the negative of the cost of the generator. In GAN, we can define a value function that the generator has to minimize and the discriminator has to maximize. The training process for a generative model is quite different from the supervised training method. GAN is sensitive to the initial weights. So we need to use batch normalization. Batch normalization makes the model stable, besides improving performance. Here, we train two models, the generative model and the discriminative model, simultaneously. Generative model G captures data distribution and discriminative model D estimates the probability of a sample that came from training data rather than G.

# GAN – code example

In the following example, we build and train a GAN model using an MNIST dataset and using TensorFlow. Here, we will use a special version of the ReLU activation function known as **Leaky ReLU**. The output is a new type of handwritten digit:

Leaky ReLU is a variation of the ReLU activation function given by the formula $f(x) = max(\alpha * x, x)$. So the output for the negative value for $x$ is *alpha* $* x$ and the output for positive $x$ is $x$.

```
#import all necessary libraries and load data set
%matplotlib inline

import pickle as pkl
import numpy as np
import tensorflow as tf
import matplotlib.pyplot as plt

from tensorflow.examples.tutorials.mnist import input_data
mnist = input_data.read_data_sets('MNIST_data')
```

In order to build this network, we need two inputs, one for the generator and one for the discriminator. In the following code, we create placeholders for `real_input` for the discriminator and `z_input` for the generator, with the input sizes as `dim_real` and `dim_z`, respectively:

```
#place holder for model inputs
def model_inputs(dim_real, dim_z):
    real_input = tf.placeholder(tf.float32, name='dim_real')
    z_input = tf.placeholder(tf.float32, name='dim_z')
    return real_input, z_input
```

Here, input `z` is a random vector to the generator which turns this vector into an image. Then we add a hidden layer, which is a leaky ReLU layer, to allow gradients to flow backwards. Leaky ReLU is just like a normal ReLU (for negative values emitting zero) except that there is a small non-zero output for negative input values. The generator performs better with the `tanhsigmoid` function. Generator output is `tanh` output. So, we'll have to rescale the MNIST images to be between -1 and 1, instead of 0 and 1. With this knowledge, we can build the generator network:

```
#Following code builds Generator Network
def generator(z, out_dim, n_units=128, reuse=False, alpha=0.01):
    ''' Build the generator network.
        Arguments
        ---------
        z : Input tensor for the generator
        out_dim : Shape of the generator output
        n_units : Number of units in hidden layer
        reuse : Reuse the variables with tf.variable_scope
        alpha : leak parameter for leaky ReLU
        Returns
        -------
        out:
    '''
    with tf.variable_scope('generator', reuse=reuse) as generator_scope: #
finish this
        # Hidden layer
        h1 = tf.layers.dense(z, n_units, activation=None )
        # Leaky ReLU
        h1 = tf.nn.leaky_relu(h1, alpha=alpha,name='leaky_generator')
        # Logits and tanh output
        logits = tf.layers.dense(h1, out_dim, activation=None)
        out = tf.tanh(logits)
        return out
```

The discriminator network is the same as the generator except that output layer is a `sigmoid` function:

```
def discriminator(x, n_units=128, reuse=False, alpha=0.01):
    ''' Build the discriminator network.
        Arguments
        ---------
        x : Input tensor for the discriminator
        n_units: Number of units in hidden layer
        reuse : Reuse the variables with tf.variable_scope
        alpha : leak parameter for leaky ReLU
        Returns
        -------
        out, logits:
    '''
    with tf.variable_scope('discriminator', reuse=reuse) as
discriminator_scope:# finish this
        # Hidden layer
        h1 = tf.layers.dense(x, n_units, activation=None )
        # Leaky ReLU
        h1 = tf.nn.leaky_relu(h1, alpha=alpha,name='leaky_discriminator')
        logits = tf.layers.dense(h1, 1, activation=None)
        out = tf.sigmoid(logits)
        return out, logits
```

To build the network, use the following code:

```
#Hyperparameters
# Size of input image to discriminator
input_size = 784 # 28x28 MNIST images flattened
# Size of latent vector to generator
z_size = 100
# Sizes of hidden layers in generator and discriminator
g_hidden_size = 128
d_hidden_size = 128
# Leak factor for leaky ReLU
alpha = 0.01
# Label smoothing
smooth = 0.1
```

We want to share weights between real and fake data, so we need to reuse the variables:

```
#Build the netwprk
tf.reset_default_graph()
# Create our input placeholders
input_real, input_z = model_inputs(input_size, z_size)

# Build the model
g_model = generator(input_z, input_size, n_units=g_hidden_size,
alpha=alpha)
# g_model is the generator output

d_model_real, d_logits_real = discriminator(input_real,
n_units=d_hidden_size, alpha=alpha)
d_model_fake, d_logits_fake = discriminator(g_model, reuse=True,
n_units=d_hidden_size, alpha=alpha)
```

# Calculating loss

For the discriminator, the total loss is the sum of the losses for real and fake images. The losses will be sigmoid cross-entropyies, which we can get using the TensorFlow `tf.nn.sigmoid_cross_entropy_with_logits`. Then we compute the mean for all the images in the batch. So the losses will look like this:

```
tf.reduce_mean(tf.nn.sigmoid_cross_entropy_with_logits(logits=logits,
labels=labels))
```

To help the discriminator generalize better, the `labels` can be reduced a bit from 1.0 to 0.9, by for example, using the parameter `smooth`. This is known as **label smoothing**, and is typically used with classifiers to improve performance. The discriminator loss for the fake data is similar. The `logits` are `d_logits_fake`, which we got from passing the generator output to the discriminator. These fake `logits` are used with `labels` of all zeros. Remember that we want the discriminator to output 1 for real images and 0 for fake images, so we need to set up the losses to reflect that.

Finally, the generator losses are using `d_logits_fake`, the fake image `logits`. But now the `labels` are all 1s. The generator is trying to fool the discriminator, so it wants the discriminator to output ones for fake images:

```
# Calculate losses
d_loss_real = tf.reduce_mean(
tf.nn.sigmoid_cross_entropy_with_logits(logits=d_logits_real,
labels=tf.ones_like(d_logits_real) * (1 - smooth)))
d_loss_fake = tf.reduce_mean(
tf.nn.sigmoid_cross_entropy_with_logits(logits=d_logits_fake,
labels=tf.zeros_like(d_logits_real)))
d_loss = d_loss_real + d_loss_fake

g_loss = tf.reduce_mean(
            tf.nn.sigmoid_cross_entropy_with_logits(logits=d_logits_fake,
labels=tf.ones_like(d_logits_fake)))
```

# Adding the optimizer

We need to update the generator and discriminator variables separately. So, first get all the variables of the graph and then, as we explained earlier, we can get only generator variables from the generator scope and, similarly, discriminator variables from the discriminator scope:

```
# Optimizers
learning_rate = 0.002

# Get the trainable_variables, split into G and D parts
t_vars = tf.trainable_variables()
g_vars = [var for var in t_vars if var.name.startswith('generator')]
d_vars = [var for var in t_vars if var.name.startswith('discriminator')]

d_train_opt = tf.train.AdamOptimizer(learning_rate).minimize(d_loss,
var_list=d_vars)
g_train_opt = tf.train.AdamOptimizer(learning_rate).minimize(g_loss,
var_list=g_vars)
```

To train the network, use:

```
batch_size = 100
epochs = 100
samples = []
losses = []
# Only save generator variables
saver = tf.train.Saver(var_list=g_vars)
with tf.Session() as sess:
```

```
        sess.run(tf.global_variables_initializer())
        for e in range(epochs):
            for ii in range(mnist.train.num_examples//batch_size):
                batch = mnist.train.next_batch(batch_size)
                # Get images, reshape and rescale to pass to D
                batch_images = batch[0].reshape((batch_size, 784))
                batch_images = batch_images*2 - 1
                # Sample random noise for G
                batch_z = np.random.uniform(-1, 1, size=(batch_size, z_size))
                # Run optimizers
                _ = sess.run(d_train_opt, feed_dict={input_real: batch_images,
input_z: batch_z})
                _ = sess.run(g_train_opt, feed_dict={input_z: batch_z})
            # At the end of each epoch, get the losses and print them out
            train_loss_d = sess.run(d_loss, {input_z: batch_z, input_real:
batch_images})
            train_loss_g = g_loss.eval({input_z: batch_z})
            print("Epoch {}/{}...".format(e+1, epochs),
                  "Discriminator Loss: {:.4f}...".format(train_loss_d),
                  "Generator Loss: {:.4f}".format(train_loss_g))
            # Save losses to view after training
            losses.append((train_loss_d, train_loss_g))
            # Sample from generator as we're training for viewing afterwards
            sample_z = np.random.uniform(-1, 1, size=(16, z_size))
            gen_samples = sess.run(
                            generator(input_z, input_size,
n_units=g_hidden_size, reuse=True, alpha=alpha),
                            feed_dict={input_z: sample_z})
            samples.append(gen_samples)
            saver.save(sess, './checkpoints/generator.ckpt')

# Save training generator samples
with open('train_samples.pkl', 'wb') as f:
    pkl.dump(samples, f)
```

Once the model is trained and saved, you can visualize the generated digits (the code is not here, but it can be downloaded).

# Semi-supervised learning and GAN

So for, we have seen how GAN can be used to generate realistic images. In this section, we will see how GAN can be used for classification tasks where we have less labeled data but still want to improve the accuracy of the classifier. Here we will also use the same **Street View House Number** or **SVHN** dataset to classify images. As previously, here we also have two networks, the generator G and discriminator D. In this case, the discriminator is trained to become a classifier. Another change is that the output of the discriminator goes to a softmax function instead of a `sigmoid` function, as seen earlier. The softmax function returns the probability distribution over labels:

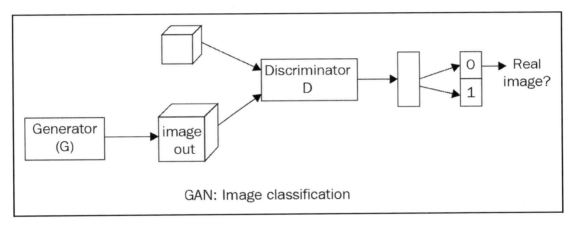

GAN: Image classification

Now we model the network as:

$$total\ cost = cost\ of\ labeled\ data + cost\ of\ unlabeled\ data$$

To get the cost of labeled data, we can use the `cross_entropy` function:

```
cost of labeled data   = cross_entropy ( logits, labels)
cost of unlabeled data =   cross_entropy ( logits, real)
```

Then we can calculate the sum of all classes:

```
real prob = sum (softmax(real_classes))
```

Normal classifiers work on labeled data. However, semi-supervised GAN-based classifiers work on labeled data, real unlabeled data, and fake images. This works very well, that is, there are less classification errors even though we have less labeled data in the training process.

# Feature matching

The idea of feature matching is to add an extra variable to the cost function of the generator in order to penalize the difference between absolute errors in the test data and training data.

# Semi-supervised classification using a GAN example

In this section, we explain how to use GAN to build a classifier with the semi-supervised learning approach.

In supervised learning, we have a training set of inputs X and class labels y. We train a model that takes X as input and gives y as output.

In semi-supervised learning, our goal is still to train a model that takes X as input and generates y as output. However, not all of our training examples have a label y.

We use the SVHN dataset. We'll turn the GAN discriminator into an 11 class discriminator (0 to 9 and one label for the fake image). It will recognize the 10 different classes of real SVHN digits, as well as an eleventh class of fake images that come from the generator. The discriminator will get to train on real labeled images, real unlabeled images, and fake images. By drawing on three sources of data instead of just one, it will generalize to the test set much better than a traditional classifier trained on only one source of data:

```
def model_inputs(real_dim, z_dim):
    inputs_real = tf.placeholder(tf.float32, (None, *real_dim),
name='input_real')
    inputs_z = tf.placeholder(tf.float32, (None, z_dim), name='input_z')
    y = tf.placeholder(tf.int32, (None), name='y')
    label_mask = tf.placeholder(tf.int32, (None), name='label_mask')
    return inputs_real, inputs_z, y, label_mask
```

## Add the generator:

```
def generator(z, output_dim, reuse=False, alpha=0.2, training=True,
size_mult=128):
    with tf.variable_scope('generator', reuse=reuse):
        # First fully connected layer
        x1 = tf.layers.dense(z, 4 * 4 * size_mult * 4)
        # Reshape it to start the convolutional stack
        x1 = tf.reshape(x1, (-1, 4, 4, size_mult * 4))
        x1 = tf.layers.batch_normalization(x1, training=training)
        x1 = tf.maximum(alpha * x1, x1)
        x2 = tf.layers.conv2d_transpose(x1, size_mult * 2, 5, strides=2,
padding='same')
        x2 = tf.layers.batch_normalization(x2, training=training)
        x2 = tf.maximum(alpha * x2, x2)
        x3 = tf.layers.conv2d_transpose(x2, size_mult, 5, strides=2,
padding='same')
        x3 = tf.layers.batch_normalization(x3, training=training)
        x3 = tf.maximum(alpha * x3, x3)
        # Output layer
        logits = tf.layers.conv2d_transpose(x3, output_dim, 5, strides=2,
padding='same')
        out = tf.tanh(logits)
        return out
```

## Add the discriminator:

```
def discriminator(x, reuse=False, alpha=0.2, drop_rate=0., num_classes=10,
size_mult=64):
    with tf.variable_scope('discriminator', reuse=reuse):
        x = tf.layers.dropout(x, rate=drop_rate/2.5)
        # Input layer is 32x32x3
        x1 = tf.layers.conv2d(x, size_mult, 3, strides=2, padding='same')
        relu1 = tf.maximum(alpha * x1, x1)
        relu1 = tf.layers.dropout(relu1, rate=drop_rate)
        x2 = tf.layers.conv2d(relu1, size_mult, 3, strides=2,
padding='same')
        bn2 = tf.layers.batch_normalization(x2, training=True)
        relu2 = tf.maximum(alpha * x2, x2)
        x3 = tf.layers.conv2d(relu2, size_mult, 3, strides=2,
padding='same')
        bn3 = tf.layers.batch_normalization(x3, training=True)
        relu3 = tf.maximum(alpha * bn3, bn3)
        relu3 = tf.layers.dropout(relu3, rate=drop_rate)
        x4 = tf.layers.conv2d(relu3, 2 * size_mult, 3, strides=1,
padding='same')
        bn4 = tf.layers.batch_normalization(x4, training=True)
        relu4 = tf.maximum(alpha * bn4, bn4)
```

```
        x5 = tf.layers.conv2d(relu4, 2 * size_mult, 3, strides=1,
    padding='same')
        bn5 = tf.layers.batch_normalization(x5, training=True)
        relu5 = tf.maximum(alpha * bn5, bn5)
        x6 = tf.layers.conv2d(relu5, 2 * size_mult, 3, strides=2,
    padding='same')
        bn6 = tf.layers.batch_normalization(x6, training=True)
        relu6 = tf.maximum(alpha * bn6, bn6)
        relu6 = tf.layers.dropout(relu6, rate=drop_rate)
        x7 = tf.layers.conv2d(relu5, 2 * size_mult, 3, strides=1,
    padding='valid')
        # Don't use bn on this layer, because bn would set the mean of each
    feature
        # to the bn mu parameter.
        # This layer is used for the feature matching loss, which only
    works if
        # the means can be different when the discriminator is run on the
    data than
        # when the discriminator is run on the generator samples.
        relu7 = tf.maximum(alpha * x7, x7)
        # Flatten it by global average pooling
        features = raise NotImplementedError()
        # Set class_logits to be the inputs to a softmax distribution over
    the different classes
        raise NotImplementedError()
        # Set gan_logits such that P(input is real | input) =
    sigmoid(gan_logits).
        # Keep in mind that class_logits gives you the probability
    distribution over all the real
        # classes and the fake class. You need to work out how to transform
    this multiclass softmax
        # distribution into a binary real-vs-fake decision that can be
    described with a sigmoid.
        # Numerical stability is very important.
        # You'll probably need to use this numerical stability trick:
        # log sum_i exp a_i = m + log sum_i exp(a_i - m).
        # This is numerically stable when m = max_i a_i.
        # (It helps to think about what goes wrong when...
        # 1. One value of a_i is very large
        # 2. All the values of a_i are very negative
        # This trick and this value of m fix both those cases, but the
    naive implementation and
        # other values of m encounter various problems)
        raise NotImplementedError()
        return out, class_logits, gan_logits, features
```

## Calculate the loss:

```
def model_loss(input_real, input_z, output_dim, y, num_classes, label_mask,
alpha=0.2, drop_rate=0.):
    """
    Get the loss for the discriminator and generator
    :param input_real: Images from the real dataset
    :param input_z: Z input
    :param output_dim: The number of channels in the output image
    :param y: Integer class labels
    :param num_classes: The number of classes
    :param alpha: The slope of the left half of leaky ReLU activation
    :param drop_rate: The probability of dropping a hidden unit
    :return: A tuple of (discriminator loss, generator loss)
    """
    # These numbers multiply the size of each layer of the generator and
the discriminator,
    # respectively. You can reduce them to run your code faster for
debugging purposes.
    g_size_mult = 32
    d_size_mult = 64
    # Here we run the generator and the discriminator
    g_model = generator(input_z, output_dim, alpha=alpha,
size_mult=g_size_mult)
    d_on_data = discriminator(input_real, alpha=alpha, drop_rate=drop_rate,
size_mult=d_size_mult)
    d_model_real, class_logits_on_data, gan_logits_on_data, data_features =
d_on_data
    d_on_samples = discriminator(g_model, reuse=True, alpha=alpha,
drop_rate=drop_rate, size_mult=d_size_mult)
    d_model_fake, class_logits_on_samples, gan_logits_on_samples,
sample_features = d_on_samples
    # Here we compute `d_loss`, the loss for the discriminator.
    # This should combine two different losses:
    # 1. The loss for the GAN problem, where we minimize the cross-entropy
for the binary
    # real-vs-fake classification problem.
    # 2. The loss for the SVHN digit classification problem, where we
minimize the cross-entropy
    # for the multi-class softmax. For this one we use the labels. Don't
forget to ignore
    # use `label_mask` to ignore the examples that we are pretending are
unlabeled for the
    # semi-supervised learning problem.
    raise NotImplementedError()
    # Here we set `g_loss` to the "feature matching" loss invented by Tim
Salimans at OpenAI.
    # This loss consists of minimizing the absolute difference between the
```

```
expected features
    # on the data and the expected features on the generated samples.
    # This loss works better for semi-supervised learning than the
tradition GAN losses.
    raise NotImplementedError()

    pred_class = tf.cast(tf.argmax(class_logits_on_data, 1), tf.int32)
    eq = tf.equal(tf.squeeze(y), pred_class)
    correct = tf.reduce_sum(tf.to_float(eq))
    masked_correct = tf.reduce_sum(label_mask * tf.to_float(eq))
    return d_loss, g_loss, correct, masked_correct, g_model
```

Add the optimizers:

```
def model_opt(d_loss, g_loss, learning_rate, beta1):
    """
    Get optimization operations
    :param d_loss: Discriminator loss Tensor
    :param g_loss: Generator loss Tensor
    :param learning_rate: Learning Rate Placeholder
    :param beta1: The exponential decay rate for the 1st moment in the
optimizer
    :return: A tuple of (discriminator training operation, generator
training operation)
    """
    # Get weights and biases to update. Get them separately for the
discriminator and the generator
    raise NotImplementedError()

    # Minimize both players' costs simultaneously
    raise NotImplementedError()
    shrink_lr = tf.assign(learning_rate, learning_rate * 0.9)
    return d_train_opt, g_train_opt, shrink_lr
```

Build the network model:

```
class GAN:
    """
    A GAN model.
    :param real_size: The shape of the real data.
    :param z_size: The number of entries in the z code vector.
    :param learnin_rate: The learning rate to use for Adam.
    :param num_classes: The number of classes to recognize.
    :param alpha: The slope of the left half of the leaky ReLU activation
    :param beta1: The beta1 parameter for Adam.
    """
    def __init__(self, real_size, z_size, learning_rate, num_classes=10,
alpha=0.2, beta1=0.5):
```

```
        tf.reset_default_graph()
        self.learning_rate = tf.Variable(learning_rate, trainable=False)
        inputs = model_inputs(real_size, z_size)
        self.input_real, self.input_z, self.y, self.label_mask = inputs
        self.drop_rate = tf.placeholder_with_default(.5, (), "drop_rate")
        loss_results = model_loss(self.input_real, self.input_z,
                                  real_size[2], self.y, num_classes,
                                  label_mask=self.label_mask,
                                  alpha=0.2,
                                  drop_rate=self.drop_rate)
        self.d_loss, self.g_loss, self.correct, self.masked_correct,
    self.samples = loss_results
        self.d_opt, self.g_opt, self.shrink_lr = model_opt(self.d_loss,
    self.g_loss, self.learning_rate, beta1)
```

Train and persist the model:

```
def train(net, dataset, epochs, batch_size, figsize=(5,5)):
    saver = tf.train.Saver()
    sample_z = np.random.normal(0, 1, size=(50, z_size))

    samples, train_accuracies, test_accuracies = [], [], []
    steps = 0

    with tf.Session() as sess:
        sess.run(tf.global_variables_initializer())
        for e in range(epochs):
            print("Epoch",e)
            t1e = time.time()
            num_examples = 0
            num_correct = 0
            for x, y, label_mask in dataset.batches(batch_size):
                assert 'int' in str(y.dtype)
                steps += 1
                num_examples += label_mask.sum()

                # Sample random noise for G
                batch_z = np.random.normal(0, 1, size=(batch_size, z_size))

                # Run optimizers
                t1 = time.time()
                _, _, correct = sess.run([net.d_opt, net.g_opt,
    net.masked_correct],
                                         feed_dict={net.input_real: x,
    net.input_z: batch_z,
                                                    net.y : y,
    net.label_mask : label_mask})
                t2 = time.time()
```

```
        num_correct += correct

    sess.run([net.shrink_lr])
    train_accuracy = num_correct / float(num_examples)
    print("\t\tClassifier train accuracy: ", train_accuracy)
    num_examples = 0
    num_correct = 0
    for x, y in dataset.batches(batch_size, which_set="test"):
        assert 'int' in str(y.dtype)
        num_examples += x.shape[0]

        correct, = sess.run([net.correct],
feed_dict={net.input_real: x,

                                    net.y : y,
                                    net.drop_rate: 0.})
        num_correct += correct
    test_accuracy = num_correct / float(num_examples)
    print("\t\tClassifier test accuracy", test_accuracy)
    print("\t\tStep time: ", t2 - t1)
    t2e = time.time()
    print("\t\tEpoch time: ", t2e - t1e)
    gen_samples = sess.run(
                    net.samples,
                    feed_dict={net.input_z: sample_z})
    samples.append(gen_samples)
    _ = view_samples(-1, samples, 5, 10, figsize=figsize)
    plt.show()
    # Save history of accuracies to view after training
    train_accuracies.append(train_accuracy)
    test_accuracies.append(test_accuracy)

    saver.save(sess, './checkpoints/generator.ckpt')

with open('samples.pkl', 'wb') as f:
    pkl.dump(samples, f)
return train_accuracies, test_accuracies, samples
```

# Deep convolutional GAN

**Deep convolutional GAN**, also called **DCGAN**, is used to generate color images. Here we use a convolutional layer in the generator and discriminator. We'll also need to use batch normalization to get the GAN to train appropriately. We will discuss batch normalization in detail in the performance improvement of deep neural networks chapter. We'll be training GAN on the SVHN dataset; a small example is shown in the following figure. After training, the generator will be able to create images that are nearly identical to these images.

You can download the code for this example:

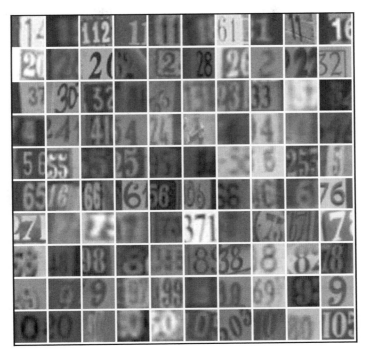

Google Street View house numbers view

# Batch normalization

Batch normalization is a technique for improving the performance and stability of neural networks. The idea is to normalize the layer inputs so that they have a mean of zero and variance of 1. Batch normalization was introduced in Sergey Ioffe's and Christian Szegedy's 2015 paper, *Batch Normalization is Necessary to Make DCGANs Work*. The idea is that instead of just normalizing the inputs to the network, we normalize the inputs to layers within the network. It's called **batch normalization** because during training, we normalize each layer's input by using the mean and variance of the values in the current mini-batch.

# Summary

In this chapter, we have seen how the GAN model truly displays the power of CNN. We learned how to train our own generative model and saw a practical example of GAN that can generate photos from paintings and turn horses into zebras.

We understood how GAN differs from other discriminative models and learned why generative models are preferred.

In the next chapter, we will learn about deep learning software comparison from scratch.

# 9

# Attention Mechanism for CNN and Visual Models

Not everything in an image or text—or in general, any data—is equally relevant from the perspective of insights that we need to draw from it. For example, consider a task where we are trying to predict the next word in a sequence of a verbose statement like *Alice and Alya are friends. Alice lives in France and works in Paris. Alya is British and works in London. Alice prefers to buy books written in French, whereas Alya prefers books in _____.*

When this example is given to a human, even a child with decent language proficiency can very well predict the next word will most probably be *English*. Mathematically, and in the context of deep learning, this can similarly be ascertained by creating a vector embedding of these words and then computing the results using vector mathematics, as follows:

$$V(\overrightarrow{Word}) = V(\overrightarrow{French}) - V(\overrightarrow{Paris}) + V(\overrightarrow{London})$$

Here, *V(Word)* is the vector embedding for the required word; similarly, *V(French)*, *V(Paris)*, and *V(London)* are the required vector embeddings for the words *French*, *Paris*, and *London*, respectively.

 Embeddings are (often) lower dimensional and dense (numerical) vector representations of inputs or indexes of inputs (for non-numerical data); in this case, text.

Algorithms such as Word2Vec and glove can be used to get word embeddings. Pretrained variants of these models for general texts are available in popular Python-based NLP libraries, such as SpaCy, Gensim and others can also be trained using most deep learning libraries, such as Keras, TensorFlow, and so on.

The concept of embeddings is as much relevant to vision and images as it is to text.

There may not be an existing vector exactly matching the vector we obtained just now in the form of $V(\overrightarrow{Word})$; but if we try to find the one closest to the so obtained $V(\overrightarrow{Word})$ that exists and find the representative word using reverse indexing, that word would most likely be the same as what we as humans thought of earlier, that is, *English*.

Algorithms such as cosine similarity can be used to get the vector closest to the computed one.

For implementation, a computationally more efficient way of finding the closest vector would be **approximate nearest neighbor** (**ANN**), as available in Python's annoy library.

Though we have helped get the same results, both cognitively and through deep learning approaches, the input in both the cases was not the same. To humans, we had given the exact sentence as to the computer, but for deep learning applications, we had carefully picked the correct words (*French*, *Paris*, and *London*) and their right position in the equation to get the results. Imagine how we can very easily realize the right words to pay attention to in order to understand the correct context, and hence we have the results; but in the current form, it was not possible for our deep learning approach to do the same.

Now there are quite sophisticated algorithms in language modeling using different variants and architectures of RNN, such as LSTM and Seq2Seq, respectively. These could have solved this problem and got the right solution, but they are most effective in shorter and more direct sentences, such as *Paris is to French what London is to* _____. In order to correctly understand a long sentence and generate the correct result, it is important to have a mechanism to teach the architecture whereby specific words need to be paid more attention to in a long sequence of words. This is called the **attention mechanism** in deep learning, and it is applicable to many types of deep learning applications but in slightly different ways.

**RNN** stands for **recurrent neural networks** and is used to depict a temporal sequence of data in deep learning. Due to the vanishing gradient problem, RNN is seldom used directly; instead, its variants, such as **LSTM (Long-Short Term Memory)** and **GRU (Gated Recurrent Unit)** are more popular in actual implementations.

**Seq2Seq** stands for **Sequence-to-Sequence** models and comprises two RNN (or variant) networks (hence it is called **Seq2Seq**, where each RNN network represents a sequence); one acts as an encoder and the other as a decoder. The two RNN networks can be multi-layer or stacked RNN networks, and they are connected via a thought or context vector. Additionally, Seq2Seq models may use the attention mechanism to improve performance, especially for longer sequences.

In fact, to be more precise, even we had to process the preceding information in layers, first understanding that the last sentence is about Alya. Then we can identify and extract Alya's city, then that for Alice, and so on. Such a layered way of human thinking is analogous to stacking in deep learning, and hence in similar applications, stacked architectures are quite common.

To know more about how stacking works in deep learning, especially with sequence-based architectures, explore topics such as stacked RNN and stacked attention networks.

In this chapter, we will cover the following topics:

- Attention mechanism for image captioning
- Types of attention (Hard, and Soft Attentions)
- Using attention to improve visual models
  - Recurrent models of visual attention

# Attention mechanism for image captioning

From the introduction, so far, it must be clear to you that the attention mechanism works on a sequence of objects, assigning each element in the sequence a weight for a specific iteration of a required output. With every next step, not only the sequence but also the weights in the attention mechanism can change. So, attention-based architectures are essentially sequence networks, best implemented in deep learning using RNNs (or their variants).

The question now is: how do we implement a sequence-based attention on a static image, especially the one represented in a **convolutional neural network** (**CNN**)? Well, let's take an example that sits right in between a text and image to understand this. Assume that we need to caption an image with respect to its contents.

We have some images with captions provided by humans as training data and using this, we need to create a system that can provide a decent caption for any new image not seen earlier by the model. As seen earlier, let's take an example and see how we, as humans, will perceive this task and the analogous process to it that needs to be implemented in deep learning and CNN. Let's consider the following image and conceive some plausible captions for it. We'll also rank them heuristically using human judgment:

Some probable captions (in order of most likely to least likely) are:

- Woman seeing dog in snow forest
- Brown dog in snow
- A person wearing cap in woods and white land
- Dog, tree, snow, person, and sunshine

An important thing to note here is that, despite the fact that the woman is central to the image and the dog is not the biggest object in the image, the caption we sought probable focused on them and then their surroundings here. This is because we consider them as important entities here (given no prior context). So as humans, how we reached this conclusion is as follows: we first glanced the whole image, and then we focused towards the woman, in high resolution, while putting everything in the background (assume a **Bokeh** effect in a dual-camera phone). We identified the caption part for that, and then the dog in high resolution while putting everything else in low resolution; and we appended the caption part. Finally, we did the same for the surroundings and caption part for that.

So essentially, we saw it in this sequence to reach to the first caption:

Image 1: Glance the image first

Image 2: Focus on woman

Image 3: Focus on dog

Image 4: Focus on snow

Image 5: Focus on forest

In terms of weight of attention or focus, after glancing the image, we focus on the first most important object: the woman here. This is analogous to creating a mental frame in which we put the part of the image with the woman in high-resolution and the remaining part of the image in low-resolution.

In a deep learning reference, the attention sequence will have the highest weight for the vector (embedding) representing the concept of the woman for this part of the sequence. In the next step of the output/sequence, the weight will shift more towards the vector representation for the dog and so on.

To understand this intuitively, we convert the image represented in the form of CNN into a flattened vector or some other similar structure; then we create different splices of the image or sequences with different parts in varying resolutions. Also, as we understand now from our discussion in `Chapter 7`, *Object-Detection & Instance-Segmentation with CNN*, we must have the relevant portions that we need to detect in varying scales as well for effective detection. The same concept applies here too, and besides resolution, we also vary the scale; but for now, we will keep it simple and ignore the scale part for intuitive understanding.

These splices or sequences of images now act as a sequence of words, as in our earlier example, and hence they can be treated inside an RNN/LSTM or similar sequence-based architecture for the purpose of attention. This is done to get the best-suited word as the output in every iteration. So the first iteration of the sequence leads to woman (from the weights of a sequence representing an object represented as a *Woman* in *Image 2*) → then the next iteration as → *seeing* (from a sequence identifying the back of the *Woman* as in *Image 2*) → *Dog* (sequence as in *Image 3*) → *in* (from a sequence where everything is blurred generating *filler* words transitioning from entities to surroundings) → *Snow* (sequence as in *Image 4*) → *Forest* (sequence as in *Image 5*).

Filler words such as *in* and action words such as *seeing* can also be automatically learned when the best image splice/sequence mapping to human-generated captions is done across several images. But for the simpler version, a caption such as *Woman, Dog, Snow,* and *Forest* can also be a good depiction of entities and surroundings in the image.

# Types of Attention

There are two types attention mechanisms. They are as follows:

- Hard attention
- Soft attention

Let's now take a look at each one in detail in the following sections.

# Hard Attention

In reality, in our recent image caption example, several more pictures would be selected, but due to our training with the handwritten captions, those would never be weighted higher. However, the essential thing to understand is how the system would understand what all pixels (or more precisely, the CNN representations of them) the system focuses on to draw these high-resolution images of different aspects and then how to choose the next pixel to repeat the process.

In the preceding example, the points are chosen at random from a distribution and the process is repeated. Also, which pixels around this point get a higher resolution is decided inside the attention network. This type of attention is known as **hard attention**.

Hard attention has something called the **differentiability problem**. Let's spend some time understanding this. We know that in deep learning the networks have to be trained and to train them we iterate across training batches in order to minimize the loss function. We can minimize the loss function by changing the weights in the direction of the gradient of the minima, which in turn is arrived at after differentiating the loss function.

This process of minimizing losses across layers of a deep network, starting from the last layer to the first, is known as **back-propagation**.

Examples of some differentiable loss functions used in deep learning and machine learning are the log-likelihood loss function, squared-error loss function, binomial and multinominal cross-entropy, and so on.

However, since the points are chosen randomly in each iteration in hard attention—and since such a random pixel choosing mechanism is not a differentiable function—we essentially cannot train this attention mechanism, as explained. This problem is overcome either by using **Reinforcement Learning** (RL) or by switching to soft attention.

RL involves mechanisms of solving two problems, either separately or in combination. The first is called the **control problem**, which determines the most optimal action that the agent should take in each step given its state, and the second is the **prediction problem**, which determines the optimal *value* of the state.

# Soft Attention

As introduced in the preceding sub-section on hard attention, soft attention uses RL to progressively train and determine where to seek next (control problem).

There exist two major problems with using the combination of hard attention and RL to achieve the required objective:

- It becomes slightly complicated to involve RL and train an RL agent and an RNN/deep network based on it separately.
- The variance in the gradient of the policy function is not only high (as in **A3C** model), but also has a computational complexity of $O(N)$, where $N$ is the number of units in the network. This increases the computation load for such approaches massively. Also, given that the attention mechanism adds more value in overly long sequences (of words or image embedding splices)—and to train networks involving longer sequences requires larger memory, and hence much deeper networks—this approach is computationally not very efficient.

The **Policy Function** in RL, determined as $Q(a,s)$, is the function used to determine the optimal policy or the action $(a)$ that should be taken in any given state $(s)$ to maximize the rewards.

So what is the alternative? As we discussed, the problem arose because the mechanism that we were choosing for attention led to a non-differentiable function, because of which we had to go with RL. So let's take a different approach here. Taking an analogy of our language modeling problem example (as in the *Attention Mechanism - Intuition* section) earlier, we assume that we have the vector of the tokens for the objects/ words present in the attention network. Also, in same vector space (say in the embedding hyperspace) we bring the tokens for the object/ words in the required query of the particular sequence step. On taking this approach, finding the right attention weights for the tokens in the attention network with the respect to the tokens in query space is as easy as computing the vector similarity between them; for example, a cosine distance. Fortunately, most vector distance and similarity functions are differentiable; hence the loss function derived by using such vector distance/similarity functions in such space is also differentiable, and our back-propagation can work in this scenario.

The cosine distance between two vectors, say $A(a1, \vec{a2}, a3)$, and $B(b1, \vec{b2}, b3)$, in a multi-dimensional (three in this example) vector space is given as:

$$Cos(\vec{A}, \vec{B}) = \frac{\vec{A}.\vec{B}}{Abs(\vec{A}) * Abs(\vec{B})} = \frac{a1b1 + a2b2 + a3c3}{\sqrt{a1^2 + a2^2 + a3^2} * \sqrt{b1^2 + b2^2 + b3^2}}$$

This approach of using a differentiable loss function for training an attention network is known as **soft attention**.

# Using attention to improve visual models

As we discovered in the NLP example covered in the earlier section on Attention Mechanism - Intuition, Attention did help us a lot in both achieving new use-cases, not optimally feasible with conventional NLP, and vastly improving the performance of the existing NLP mechanism. Similar is the usage of Attention in CNN and Visual Models as well

In the earlier chapter Chapter 7, *Object-Detection & Instance-Segmentation with CNN*, we discovered how Attention (like) mechanism are used as Region Proposal Networks for networks like Faster R-CNN and Mask R-CNN, to greatly enhance and optimize the proposed regions, and enable the generation of segment masks. This corresponds to the first part of the discussion. In this section, we will cover the second part of the discussion, where we will use 'Attention' mechanism to improve the performance of our CNNs, even under extreme conditions.

# Reasons for sub-optimal performance of visual CNN models

The performance of a CNN network can be improved to a certain extent by adopting proper tuning and setup mechanisms such as: data pre-processing, batch normalization, optimal pre-initialization of weights; choosing the correct activation function; using techniques such as regularization to avoid overfitting; using an optimal optimization function; and training with plenty of (quality) data.

Beyond these training and architecture-related decisions, there are image-related nuances because of which the performance of visual models may be impacted. Even after controlling the aforementioned training and architectural factors, the conventional CNN-based image classifier does not work well under some of the following conditions related to the underlying images:

- Very big images
- Highly cluttered images with a number of classification entities
- Very noisy images

Let's try to understand the reasons behind the sub-optimal performance under these conditions, and then we will logically understand what may fix the problem.

In conventional CNN-based models, even after a downsizing across layers, the computational complexity is quite high. In fact, the complexity is of the order of $O(L * WB * PPI^2)$, where $L$ and $W$ are the length and width of the image in inches, and $PPI$ is pixels per inch (pixel density). This translates into a linear complexity with respect to the total number of pixels ($P$) in the image, or $O(P)$. This directly answers the first point of the challenge; for higher $L$, $W$, or $PPI$, we need much higher computational power and time to train the network.

 Operations such as max-pooling, average-pooling, and so on help downsize the computational load drastically vis-a-vis all the computations across all the layers performed on the actual image.

If we visualize the patterns formed in each of the layers of our CNN, we would understand the intuition behind the working of the CNN and why it needs to be deep. In each subsequent layer, the CNN trains higher conceptual features, which may progressively better help understand the objects in the image layer after layer. So, in the case of MNIST, the first layer may only identify boundaries, the second the diagonals and straight-line-based shapes of the boundaries, and so on:

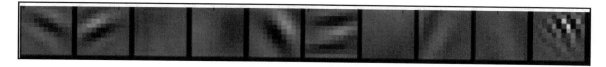

Illustrative conceptual features formed in different (initial) layers of CNN for MNIST

MNIST is a simple dataset, whereas real-life images are quite complex; this requires higher conceptual features to distinguish them, and hence more complex and much deeper networks. Moreover, in MNIST, we are trying to distinguish between similar types of objects (all handwritten numbers). Whereas in real life, the objects might differ widely, and hence the different types of features that may be required to model all such objects will be very high:

This brings us to our second challenge. A cluttered image with too many objects would require a very complex network to model all these objects. Also, since there are too many objects to identify, the image resolution needs to be good to correctly extract and map the features for each object, which in turn means that the image size and the number of pixels need to be high for an effective classification. This, in turn, increases the complexity exponentially by combining the first two challenges.

The number of layers, and hence the complexity of popular CNN architectures used in ImageNet challenges, have been increasing over the years. Some examples are VGG16 – Oxford (2014) with 16 layers, GoogLeNet (2014) with 19 layers, and ResNet (2015) with 152 layers.

Not all images are perfect SLR quality. Often, because of low light, image processing, low resolution, lack of stabilization, and so on, there may be a lot of noise introduced in the image. This is just one form of noise, one that is easier to understand. From the perspective of CNN, another form of noise can be image transition, rotation, or transformation:

Image without noise

Same image with added noise

In the preceding images, try reading the newspaper title *Business* in the image without and with noise, or identify the mobile in both the images. Difficult to do that in the image with noise, right? Similar is the detection/classification challenge with our CNN in the case of noisy images.

Even with exhaustive training, perfect hyperparameter adjustment, and techniques such as dropouts and others, these real-life challenges continue to diminish the image recognition accuracy of CNN networks. Now that we've understood the causes and intuition behind the lack of accuracy and performance in our CNNs, let's explore some ways and architectures to alleviate these challenges using visual attention.

# Recurrent models of visual attention

*Recurrent models of visual attention* can be used to answer some of the challenges we covered in the earlier section. These models use the hard attention method, as covered in an earlier (*Types of attention*) section. Here we use one of the popular variants of recurrent models of visual attention, the **Recurrent Attention Model** (**RAM**).

As covered earlier, hard attention problems are non-differentiable and have to use RL for the control problem. The RAM thus uses RL for this optimization.

A recurrent model of visual attention does not process the entire image, or even a sliding-window-based bounding box, at once. It mimics the human eye and works on the concept of *Fixation* of *Gaze* at different locations of an image; with each *Fixation*, it incrementally combines information of importance to dynamically build up an internal representation of scenes in the image. It uses an RNN to do this in a sequential manner.

The model selects the next location to Fixate to based on the RL agents control policy to maximize the reward based on the current state. The current state, in turn, is a function of all the past information and the demands of the task. Thus, it finds the next coordinate for fixation so that it can maximize the reward (demands of the task), given the information collected until now across the previous gazes in the memory snapshot of the RNN and the previously visited coordinate.

 Most RL mechanisms use the **Markov Decision Process** (**MDP**), in which the next action is determined only by the current state, irrespective of the states visited earlier. By using RNN here, important information from previous *Fixations* can be combined in the present state itself.

The preceding mechanism solves the last two problems highlighted in CNN in the earlier section. Also, in the RAM, the number of parameters and amount of computation it performs can be controlled independently of the size of the input image, thus solving the first problem as well.

# Applying the RAM on a noisy MNIST sample

To understand the working of the RAM in greater detail, let's try to create an MNIST sample incorporating some of the problems as highlighted in the earlier section:

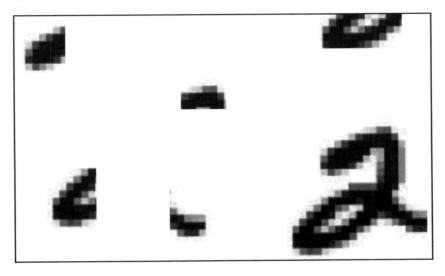

Larger image of noisy and distorted MNIST

The preceding image represents a larger image/collage using an actual and slightly noisy sample of an MNIST image (of number **2**), and a lot of other distortions and snippets of other partial samples. Also, the actual digit **2** here is not centered. This example represents all the previously stated problems, yet it is simple enough to understand the working of the RAM.

The RAM uses the concept of a **Glimpse Sensor**. The RL agent fixes its gaze at a particular coordinate (*l*) and particular time (*t-1*). The coordinate at time t-1, $l_{t-1}$ of the image $x_t$ and uses the **Glimpse Sensor** to extract retina-like multiple-resolution patches of the image with $l_{t-1}$ as the center. These representations, extracted at time *t-1*, are collectively called $p(x_t, l_{t-1})$:

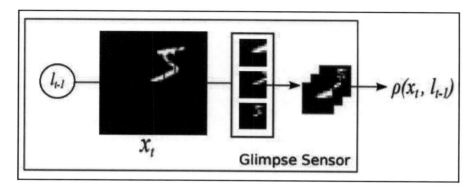

The concept of the Glimpse Sensor

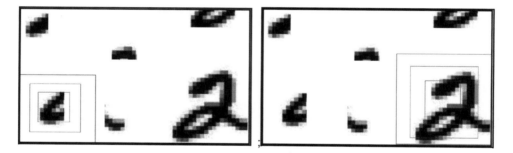

These images show the representations of our image across two fixations using the **Glimpse Sensor**.

The representations obtained from the **Glimpse Sensor** are passes through the 'Glimpse Network, which flattens the representation at two stages. In the first stage, the representations from the **Glimpse Sensor** and the **Glimpse Network** are flattened separately ($\theta_g^0, \theta_g^1$), and then they are combined into a single flattened layer ($\theta_g^2$) to generate the output representation $g_t$ for time *t*:

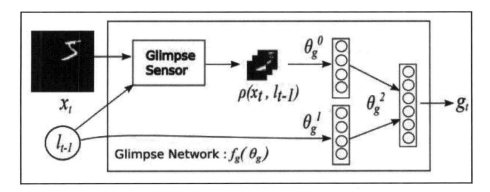

The concept of the Glimpse Network

These output representations are then passed through the RNN model architecture. The fixation for the next step in the iteration is determined by the RL agent to maximize the reward from this architecture:

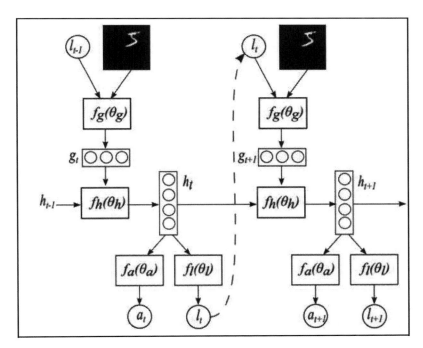

Model architecture (RNN)

As can be intuitively understood, the Glimpse Sensor captures important information across fixations, which can help identify important concepts. For example, the multiple resolution (here 3) representations at the Fixation represented by our second sample image have three resolutions as marked (red, green, and blue in order of decreasing resolution). As can be seen, even if these are used directly, we have got a varying capability to detect the right digit represented by this noisy collage:

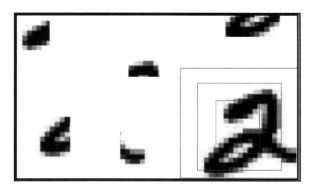

| Digit | Probability | Probability | Probability |
|---|---|---|---|
| 0 | 0.01 | 0.15 | 0.06 |
| 1 | 0.03 | 0.12 | 0.08 |
| 2 | 0.72 | 0.26 | 0.01 |
| 3 | 0.04 | 0.13 | 0.05 |
| 4 | 0.02 | 0.01 | 0.06 |
| 5 | 0.05 | 0.12 | 0.1 |
| 6 | 0.03 | 0.13 | 0.12 |
| 7 | 0.01 | 0.04 | 0.12 |
| 8 | 0.04 | 0.01 | 0.06 |
| 9 | 0.05 | 0.03 | 0.05 |

## Glimpse Sensor in code

As discussed in the earlier section, the Glimpse Sensor is a powerful concept. Combined with other concepts, such as RNN and RL, as discussed earlier, it is at the heart of improving the performance of visual models.

Let's see this in greater detail here. The code is commented at every line for easy understanding and is self-explanatory:

```python
import tensorflow as tf
# the code is in tensorflow
import numpy as np


def glimpseSensor(image, fixationLocation):
    '''
    Glimpse Sensor for Recurrent Attention Model (RAM)
    :param image: the image xt
    :type image: numpy vector
    :param fixationLocation: cordinates l for fixation center
    :type fixationLocation: tuple
    :return: Multi Resolution Representations from Glimpse Sensor
    :rtype:
    '''

    img_size=np.asarray(image).shape[:2]
    # this can be set as default from the size of images in our dataset,
leaving the third 'channel' dimension if any

    channels=1
    # settings channels as 1 by default
    if (np.asarray(img_size).shape[0]==3):
        channels=np.asarray(image).shape[-1]
    # re-setting the channel size if channels are present

    batch_size=32
    # setting batch size

    loc = tf.round(((fixationLocation + 1) / 2.0) * img_size)
    # fixationLocation coordinates are normalized between -1 and 1 wrt
image center as 0,0

    loc = tf.cast(loc, tf.int32)
    # converting number format compatible with tf

    image = tf.reshape(image, (batch_size, img_size[0], img_size[1],
channels))
    # changing img vector shape to fit tf

    representaions = []
    # representations of image
    glimpse_images = []
    # to show in window
```

```
minRadius=img_size[0]/10
# setting the side size of the smallest resolution image
max_radius=minRadius*2
offset = 2 * max_radius
# setting the max side and offset for drawing representations
depth = 3
# number of representations per fixation
sensorBandwidth = 8
# sensor bandwidth for glimpse sensor

# process each image individually
for k in range(batch_size):
    imageRepresentations = []
    one_img = image[k,:,:,:]
    # selecting the required images to form a batch

    one_img = tf.image.pad_to_bounding_box(one_img, offset, offset,
max_radius * 4 + img_size, max_radius * 4 + img_size)
    # pad image with zeros for use in tf as we require consistent size

    for i in range(depth):
        r = int(minRadius * (2 ** (i)))
        # radius of draw
        d_raw = 2 * r
        # diameter

        d = tf.constant(d_raw, shape=[1])
        # tf constant for dia

        d = tf.tile(d, [2])
        loc_k = loc[k,:]
        adjusted_loc = offset + loc_k - r
        # location wrt image adjusted wrt image transformation and pad

        one_img2 = tf.reshape(one_img, (one_img.get_shape()[0].value,
one_img.get_shape()[1].value))
        # reshaping image for tf

        representations = tf.slice(one_img2, adjusted_loc, d)
        # crop image to (d x d) for representation

        representations =
tf.image.resize_bilinear(tf.reshape(representations, (1, d_raw, d_raw, 1)),
(sensorBandwidth, sensorBandwidth))
        # resize cropped image to (sensorBandwidth x sensorBandwidth)

        representations = tf.reshape(representations, (sensorBandwidth,
sensorBandwidth))
```

```
        # reshape for tf

        imageRepresentations.append(representations)
        # appending the current representation to the set of
representations for image

        representaions.append(tf.stack(imageRepresentations))

    representations = tf.stack(representations)

    glimpse_images.append(representations)
    # return glimpse sensor output
    return representations
```

# References

1. Kelvin Xu, Jimmy Ba, Ryan Kiros, Kyunghyun Cho, Aaron C. Courville, Ruslan Salakhutdinov, Richard S. Zemel, Yoshua Bengio, Show, Attend and Tell: *Neural Image Caption Generation with Visual Attention*, CoRR, arXiv:1502.03044, 2015.

2. Karl Moritz Hermann, Tom's Kocisk, Edward Grefenstette, Lasse Espeholt, Will Kay, Mustafa Suleyman, Phil Blunsom, *Teaching Machines to Read and Comprehend*, CoRR, arXiv:1506.03340, 2015.

3. Volodymyr Mnih, Nicolas Heess, Alex Graves, Koray Kavukcuoglu, *Recurrent Models of Visual Attention*, CoRR, arXiv:1406.6247, 2014.

4. Long Chen, Hanwang Zhang, Jun Xiao, Liqiang Nie, Jian Shao, Tat-Seng Chua, SCA-CNN: *Spatial and Channel-wise Attention in Convolutional Networks for Image Captioning*, CoRR, arXiv:1611.05594, 2016.

5. Kan Chen, Jiang Wang, Liang-Chieh Chen, Haoyuan Gao, Wei Xu, Ram Nevatia, ABC-CNN: *An Attention Based Convolutional Neural Network for Visual Question Answering*, CoRR, arXiv:1511.05960, 2015.

6. Wenpeng Yin, Sebastian Ebert, Hinrich Schutze, *Attention-Based Convolutional Neural Network for Machine Comprehension*, CoRR, arXiv:1602.04341, 2016.

7. Wenpeng Yin, Hinrich Schutze, Bing Xiang, Bowen Zhou, ABCNN: *Attention-Based Convolutional Neural Network for Modeling Sentence Pairs*, CoRR, arXiv:1512.05193, 2015.

8. Zichao Yang, Xiaodong He, Jianfeng Gao, Li Deng, Alexander J. Smola, *Stacked Attention Networks for Image Question Answering*, CoRR, arXiv:1511.02274, 2015.

9. Y. Chen, D. Zhao, L. Lv and C. Li, *A visual attention based convolutional neural network for image classification*, 2016 12th World Congress on Intelligent Control and Automation (WCICA), Guilin, 2016, pp. 764-769.

10. H. Zheng, J. Fu, T. Mei and J. Luo, *Learning Multi-attention Convolutional Neural Network for Fine-Grained Image Recognition*, 2017 IEEE International Conference on Computer Vision (ICCV), Venice, 2017, pp. 5219-5227.

11. Tianjun Xiao, Yichong Xu, Kuiyuan Yang, Jiaxing Zhang, Yuxin Peng, Zheng Zhang, *The Application of Two-level Attention Models in Deep Convolutional Neural Network for Fine-grained Image Classification*, CoRR, arXiv:1411.6447, 2014.

12. Jlindsey15, *A TensorFlow implementation of the recurrent attention model*, GitHub, https://github.com/jlindsey15/RAM, Feb 2018.

13. QihongL, *A TensorFlow implementation of the recurrent attention model*, GitHub, https://github.com/QihongL/RAM, Feb 2018.

14. Amasky, *Recurrent Attention Model*, GitHub, https://github.com/amasky/ram, Feb 2018.

# Summary

The attention mechanism is the hottest topic in deep learning today and is conceived to be in the center of most of the cutting-edge algorithms under current research, and in probable future applications. Problems such as image captioning, visual question answering, and many more have gotten great solutions by using this approach. In fact, attention is not limited to visual tasks and was conceived earlier for problems such as neural machine translations and other sophisticated NLP problems. Thus, understanding the attention mechanism is vital to mastering many advanced deep learning techniques.

CNNs are used not only for vision but also for many good applications with attention for solving complex NLP problems, such as **modeling sentence pairs and machine translation**. This chapter covered the attention mechanism and its application to some NLP problems, along with image captioning and recurrent vision models. In RAMs, we did not use CNN; instead, we applied RNN and attention to reduced-size representations of an image from the Glimpse Sensor. But there are recent works to apply attention to CNN-based visual models as well.

Readers are highly encouraged to go through the original papers in the references and also explore advanced concepts in using attention, such as multi-level attention, stacked attention models, and the use of RL models (such as the **Asynchronous Advantage Actor-Critic (A3C)** model for the hard attention control problem).

# Other Books You May Enjoy

If you enjoyed this book, you may be interested in these other books by Packt:

**Neural Network Programming with Tensorflow**
Rajdeep Dua, Manpreet Singh Ghotra

ISBN: 978-1-78839-039-2

- Learn Linear Algebra and mathematics behind neural network.
- Dive deep into Neural networks from the basic to advanced concepts like CNN, RNN Deep Belief Networks, Deep Feedforward Networks.
- Explore Optimization techniques for solving problems like Local minima, Global minima, Saddle points
- Learn through real world examples like Sentiment Analysis.
- Train different types of generative models and explore autoencoders.
- Explore TensorFlow as an example of deep learning implementation.

## TensorFlow 1.x Deep Learning Cookbook
Antonio Gulli, Amita Kapoor

ISBN: 978-1-78829-359-4

- Install TensorFlow and use it for CPU and GPU operations
- Implement DNNs and apply them to solve different AI-driven problems.
- Leverage different data sets such as MNIST, CIFAR-10, and Youtube8m with TensorFlow and learn how to access and use them in your code.
- Use TensorBoard to understand neural network architectures, optimize the learning process, and peek inside the neural network black box.
- Use different regression techniques for prediction and classification problems
- Build single and multilayer perceptrons in TensorFlow
- Implement CNN and RNN in TensorFlow, and use it to solve real-world use cases.
- Learn how restricted Boltzmann Machines can be used to recommend movies.
- Understand the implementation of Autoencoders and deep belief networks, and use them for emotion detection.
- Master the different reinforcement learning methods to implement game playing agents.
- GANs and their implementation using TensorFlow.

# Leave a review - let other readers know what you think

Please share your thoughts on this book with others by leaving a review on the site that you bought it from. If you purchased the book from Amazon, please leave us an honest review on this book's Amazon page. This is vital so that other potential readers can see and use your unbiased opinion to make purchasing decisions, we can understand what our customers think about our products, and our authors can see your feedback on the title that they have worked with Packt to create. It will only take a few minutes of your time, but is valuable to other potential customers, our authors, and Packt. Thank you!

# Index

Printed in Great Britain
by Amazon